EVERYMAN,
I WILL GO WITH THEE
AND BE THY GUIDE,
IN THY MOST NEED
TO GO BY THY SIDE

EVERYMAN'S LIBRARY
POCKET POETS

POEMS

OF THE

AMERICAN
SOUTH

·

EDITED BY

DAVID BIESPIEL

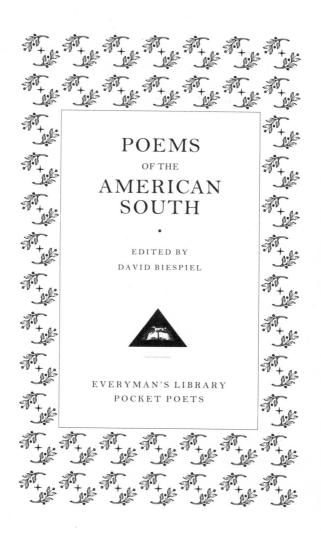

EVERYMAN'S LIBRARY
POCKET POETS

THIS IS A BORZOI BOOK
PUBLISHED BY ALFRED A. KNOPF

This selection by David Biespiel first published in
Everyman's Library, 2014
Copyright © 2014 by Everyman's Library

A list of acknowledgments to copyright owners appears at the back
of this volume.

All rights reserved. Published in the United States by Alfred A. Knopf,
a division of Random House LLC, New York, a division of Penguin
Random House Companies and in Canada by Random House of Canada
Limited, Toronto. Distributed by Random House LLC, New York.
Published in the United Kingdom by Everyman's Library, Northburgh
House, 10 Northburgh Street, London EC1V 0AT and distributed by
Random House (UK) Ltd.

www.randomhouse.com/everymans
www.everymanslibrary.co.uk

ISBN 978-0-375-71244-9 (US)
978-1-84159-795-9 (UK)

A CIP catalogue record for this book is available from the British Library

Typography by Peter B. Willberg
Typeset in the UK by AccComputing, Wincanton, Somerset
Printed and bound in Germany by GGP Media GmbH, Pössneck

CONTENTS

BAYOU AND THE LONE STAR

A CLOUD OF WITNESSES

DESTINATIONS AND TENDER MERCIES

FOREWORD

No other region in America is as mythologized as the South. It can at times be a troubled narration. The South was founded on a scheme of brutal slavery, aggrieved by civil war, glorified by a false lost cause, and shackled to legalized racial segregation. A Southerner's soul-searching has long been one of agitation and anguish, chagrin and disquiet, a harrowed and mortified and tormented weave.

Running boldly beneath that narrative, on the other hand, is a heartbeat of liberty and equity too: the Virginia Statute for Religious Freedom and the White Sulphur Manifesto, the Underground Railroad and the Freedom Riders, the Montgomery Bus Boycott and the Letter from Birmingham Jail.

These histories have now met a new, defining reality in the South, a phenomenon prevalent across the United States. The white baby-boom generation is nearing retirement and the new generation of Southerners is made up of a growing population of African Americans, Asians, Hispanics, and people of all races, blended into a melting pot of accelerating economic change. This demographic shift is at the root of a renewed vibrancy in political life in the American South, and it is at the root of a renewed vibrancy in the poetry of the American South as well.

But the South's self-mythologizing is not just restricted to economic and political history. Southern culture is American culture. Southerners are proud of inventing American music — jazz and the blues, bluegrass and gospel, country and western and zydeco. Southerners are proud of inventing a diverse American cuisine — corn bread and shoofly and succotash, grits and chicken fried steak, BBQ, bourbon, and red-eye gravy.

When it comes to ruminating and swapping stories about the South, Southerners will bless and eulogize, fret and lionize, despair and glorify. As a Texan, I dearly love my home state with all its perplexing incongruities. I consider my love, as Molly Ivins once put it, "a harmless perversion on my part, and discuss it only with consenting adults."

These dynamic renditions of the South evoke country swamps and suburban malls, lost byways and ten-lane freeways, rednecks and yuppies and snowbirds. Given the ease with which one can summon the totems of the South, and given the way that the culture and history of the South serves as an emotional lightning rod across the nation, at times unfairly, it's worth asking what can be said about the South that hasn't been said already?

And yet: even if it seems that nothing new can be said, that's precisely where poetry steps in. More to the point, poetry *must* step in because poetry's calling is to say the new thing. It is the art of finding new words in new orders. It is poetic utterance that dramatizes afresh the inner consciousness and outer stories of our existence.

This ambition holds true for the poetry of the American South as well. Here I mean to emphasize the *of* and not just the *South* in that formulation. This anthology begins with the hymns and rhythms of enslaved people who were shipped to this continent four hundred years ago against their will. Enslaved Africans brought with them the roots of American poetry and, as a consequence, there's been an ingrained sensibility about the tragedy of human bondage in Southern literature; as William Faulkner famously said, "The past is not dead. It isn't even past."

If these essential poems of enslaved Africans, which date back to the eighteenth century, present a profound moral stance on subjugation and deliverance, the poetry written by nineteenth-century Southern poets is marked by piousness baked into inflated nostalgia. These are voices that burn for the doomed Confederacy, pine for antebellum mush, and are filled to the brim with patriotic camp.

Without reading this post-Civil War verse, however, a sense of the distance contemporary poetry has come in its relation to the Old South would be harder to detect. For one thing, these archaic, post-war bromides

13

so reeked of lame-brained schmaltz that they alienated the early twentieth-century Southern modernists, known as the Fugitives, who took up the task of debating Southern identity. In so doing, these poets – John Crowe Ransom, Robert Penn Warren, and others – created an American art of rediscovery. For another thing, today early twenty-first-century Southern poetry is filigreed both with the traditional pull of the past and with the contemporary pull of individual consciousness. "Go straight to the things that make your own existence exist," James Dickey once wrote, a dictum that has found its way into the hearts of our new poets.

However, *Poems of the American South* is not just a book of poems by Southerners. In our time, the very notion of regional poetry is problematic. Geographic mobility may be on the decline across the United States, but ease of travel has put the South up for grabs as a subject for poets from all over.

Alongside poems by Southerners, you will find here poems by Northerners and Westerners and Midwesterners – that is, poems *of* the South. You'll find Elizabeth Bishop in Florida and a magnolia tree in New Jersey, Walt Whitman looking past Dixie, and Hart Crane, too. You'll find the bard of Harlem, Langston Hughes, characterizing Southern racial experience in a way that has inspired generations of poets, regardless of their race, to re-examine what it means to live in a racially mixed world. You'll find contemporary African American and Hispanic poets defining the South with a verve that is redefining American poetry as a whole.

You'll find places to recognize anew as well: the Hill Country and the Low Country, Metrolina and Metro Dade, Northern Neck and Pee Dee, Piedmont Triad and the Quad Cities.

But I feel remiss. Reading poetry is not just reading in order to locate the subject of a poem on a map.

A poem is not made up just of analogues, denotations, and renditions of experiences, facts, and geographic places. "I am looking for a way to vocalize, perform, act out, address the commonly felt crises of my time," C. D. Wright, who was born in Arkansas, has said about the spiritual bloodline of poetry. "You know a good poem by whether or not those irreducible dark spots are integral to your experience as a whole," Christian Wiman, who was born in Texas, has said. And Natasha Trethewey, who was born in Mississippi and now lives in Georgia, says, "No matter how people think about poetry or think they think about it on a regular basis, people turn to it in some of the most trying times in our lives. We also turn to it in times of triumph and joy."

The poems included here are revelatory. They are like wish fulfillments full of unknowing. I believe they will nourish and delight you. They are poems of the past and of our time – and, yes, also of a geographic and psychic place. Above all, they embody a spirit of rediscovery that is meant to be historic, contemporary, and timeless.

DAVID BIESPIEL

SONGS OF FREEDOM

Where're you bound?
Bound for Canaan land

BOUND FOR CANAAN LAND

Where're you bound?
Bound for Canaan land

O, you must not lie
You must not steal
You must not take God's name in vain
I'm bound for Canaan land

Your horse is white, your garment is bright
You look like a man of war
Raise up your head with courage bold
For your race is almost run

How you know?
Jesus told me

Although you see me going so
I'm bound for Canaan land
I have trials here below
I'm bound for Canaan land

NOBODY KNOWS DE TROUBLE I'VE HAD

Nobody knows de trouble I've had
Nobody knows but Jesus
Nobody knows de trouble I've had
Glory, hallelu!

One morning I was a-walking down
O yes, Lord
I saw some berries a-hanging down
O yes, Lord

Nobody knows de trouble I've had
Nobody knows but Jesus
Nobody knows de trouble I've had
Glory, hallelu!

I pick de berry and I suck de juice
O yes, Lord
Just as sweet as the honey in de comb
O yes, Lord

Nobody knows de trouble I've had
Nobody knows but Jesus
Nobody knows de trouble I've had
Glory, hallelu!

Sometimes I'm up, sometimes I'm down
O yes, Lord
Sometimes I'm almost o de groun'.
O yes, Lord

Nobody knows de trouble I've had
Nobody knows but Jesus
Nobody knows de trouble I've had
Glory, hallelu!

What make ole Saten hate me so
O yes, Lord
Because he got me once and he let me go
O yes, Lord

Nobody knows de trouble I've had
Nobody knows but Jesus
Nobody knows de trouble I've had
Glory, hallelu!

THE GOOD OLD WAY

As I went down in de valley to pray,
Studying about dat good old way,
When you shall wear de starry crown,
Good Lord, show me de way.

O mourner, let's go down,
Let's go down, let's go down.
O mourner, let's go down,
Down in de valley to pray.

GO TO SLEEP

Go to sleep, go to sleep
Go to sleep, little baby
Mama gone away
An' papa gone, too.
Go to sleep, little baby.

Go to sleep, go to sleep
Go to sleep, little baby
Mama gone away
An' daddy, too.
Go to sleep, little baby.

LOOKOUTS

O magnet-south! O glistening perfumed South! my South!
— WALT WHITMAN

SOUTHERN CROSS
From *The Bridge*

I wanted you, nameless Woman of the South,
No wraith, but utterly – as still more alone
The Southern Cross takes night
And lifts her girdles from her, one by one –
High, cool,
                    wide from the slowly smoldering fire
Of lower heavens, –
                              vaporous scars!

Eve! Magdalene!
                    or Mary, you?

Whatever call – falls vainly on the wave.
O simian Venus, homeless Eve,
Unwedded, stumbling gardenless to grieve
Windswept guitars on lonely decks forever;
Finally to answer all within one grave!

And this long wake of phosphor,
                                        iridescent
Furrow of all our travel – trailed derision!
Eyes crumble at its kiss. Its long-drawn spell
Incites a yell. Slid on that backward vision
The mind is churned to spittle, whispering hell.

I wanted you . . . The embers of the Cross
Climbed by aslant and huddling aromatically.
It is blood to remember; it is fire
To stammer back . . . It is
God – your namelessness. And the wash –

All night the water combed you with black
Insolence. You crept out simmering, accomplished.
Water rattled that stinging coil, your
Rehearsed hair – docile, alas, from many arms.
Yes, Eve – wraith of my unloved seed!

The Cross, a phantom, buckled – dropped below
    the dawn.
Light drowned the lithic trillions of your spawn.

THE SOUTH

The lazy, laughing South
With blood on its mouth.
The sunny-faced South,
      Beast-strong,
      Idiot-brained.
The child-minded South
Scratching in the dead fire's ashes
For a Negro's bones.
      Cotton and the moon,
      Warmth, earth, warmth,
      The sky, the sun, the stars,
      The magnolia-scented South.
Beautiful, like a woman,
Seductive as a dark-eyed whore,
      Passionate, cruel,
      Honey-lipped, syphilitic –
      That is the South.
And I, who am black, would love her
But she spits in my face.
And I, who am black,
Would give her many rare gifts
But she turns her back upon me.
      So now I seek the North –
      The cold-faced North,
      For she, they say,

Is a kinder mistress,
And in her house my children
May escape the spell of the South.

REVERIE IN OPEN AIR

I acknowledge my status as a stranger:
Inappropriate clothes, odd habits
Out of sync with wasp and wren.
I admit I don't know how
To sit still or move without purpose.
I prefer books to moonlight, statuary to trees.

But this lawn has been leveled for looking,
So I kick off my sandals and walk its cool green.
Who claims we're mere muscle and fluids?
My feet are the primitives here.
As for the rest – ah, the air now
Is a tonic of absence, bearing nothing
But news of a breeze.

RITA DOVE (1952–)   31

PASTORAL

In the dream, I am with the Fugitive
Poets. We're gathered for a photograph.
Behind us, the skyline of Atlanta
hidden by the photographer's backdrop –
a lush pasture, green, full of soft-eyed cows
lowing, a chant that sounds like *no, no. Yes,*
I say to the glass of bourbon I'm offered.
We're lining up now – Robert Penn Warren,
his voice just audible above the drone
of bulldozers, telling us where to stand.
Say "race," the photographer croons. I'm in
blackface again when the flash freezes us.
My father's white, I tell them, *and rural.*
You don't hate the South? they ask. *You don't hate it?*

TAR HEEL AND PALMETTO

POEMS OF NORTH AND SOUTH CAROLINA

DEFENCE OF FORT McHENRY

O! say can you see, by the dawn's early light,
What so proudly we hail'd at the twilight's last
    gleaming,
Whose broad stripes and bright stars through the
    perilous fight,
O'er the ramparts we watch'd, were so gallantly
    streaming?
And the rockets' red glare, the bombs bursting in air,
Gave proof through the night that our flag was still
    there –
O! say, does that star-spangled banner yet wave
O'er the land of the free, and the home of the brave?

On the shore, dimly seen through the mists of the deep,
Where the foe's haughty host in dread silence reposes,
What is that which the breeze o'er the towering steep,
As it fitfully blows, half conceals, half discloses?
Now it catches the gleam of the morning's first beam,
In full glory reflected now shines on the stream –
'Tis the star-spangled banner, O! long may it wave
O'er the land of the free, and the home of the brave.

And where is that band who so vauntingly swore
That the havoc of war and the battle's confusion
A home and a country should leave us no more?

Their blood has wash'd out their foul foot-steps'
    pollution,
No refuge could save the hireling and slave,
From the terror of flight or the gloom of the grave;
And the star-spangled banner in triumph doth wave
O'er the land of the free, and the home of the brave.

O! thus be it ever when freemen shall stand
Between their lov'd home, and the war's desolation,
Blest with vict'ry and peace, may the heav'n-rescued
    land
Praise the power that hath made and preserv'd us a
    nation!
Then conquer we must, when our cause it is just,
And this be our motto – "In God is our trust!"
And the star-spangled banner in triumph shall wave
O'er the land of the free, and the home of the brave.

EASTER MORNING

I have a life that did not become,
that turned aside and stopped,
astonished:
I hold it in me like a pregnancy or
as on my lap a child
not to grow or grow old but dwell on

it is to his grave I most
frequently return and return
to ask what is wrong, what was
wrong, to see it all by
the light of a different necessity
but the grave will not heal
and the child,
stirring, must share my grave
with me, an old man having
gotten by on what was left

when I go back to my home country in these
fresh far-away days, it's convenient to visit
everybody, aunts and uncles, those who used to say,
look how he's shooting up, and the
trinket aunts who always had a little
something in their pocketbooks, cinnamon bark
or a penny or nickel, and uncles who
were the rumored fathers of cousins

who whispered of them as of great, if
troubled, presences, and school
teachers, just about everybody older
(and some younger) collected in one place
waiting, particularly, but not for
me, mother and father there, too, and others
close, close as burrowing
under skin, all in the graveyard
assembled, done for, the world they
used to wield, have trouble and joy
in, gone

the child in me that could not become
was not ready for others to go,
to go on into change, blessings and
horrors, but stands there by the road
where the mishap occurred, crying out for
help, come and fix this or we
can't get by, but the great ones who
were to return, they could not or did
not hear and went on in a flurry and
now, I say in the graveyard, here
lies the flurry, now it can't come
back with help or helpful asides, now
we all buy the bitter
incompletions, pick up the knots of
horror, silently raving, and go on

crashing into empty ends not
completions, not rondures the fullness
has come into and spent itself from

I stand on the stump
of a child, whether myself
or my little brother who died, and
yell as far as I can, I cannot leave this place, for
for me it is the dearest and the worst,
it is life nearest to life which is
life lost: it is my place where
I must stand and fail,
calling attention with tears
to the branches not lofting
boughs into space, to the barren
air that holds the world that was my world

though the incompletions
(& completions) burn out
standing in the flash high-burn
momentary structure of ash, still it
is a picture-book, letter-perfect
Easter morning: I have been for a
walk: the wind is tranquil: the brook
works without flashing in an abundant
tranquility: the birds are lively with
voice: I saw something I had
never seen before: two great birds,

maybe eagles, blackwinged, whitenecked
and -headed, came from the south oaring
the great wings steadily; they went
directly over me, high up, and kept on
due north: but then one bird,
the one behind, veered a little to the
left and the other bird kept on seeming
not to notice for a minute: the first
began to circle as if looking for
something, coasting, resting its wings
on the down side of some of the circles:
the other bird came back and they both
circled, looking perhaps for a draft;
they turned a few more times, possibly
rising – at least, clearly resting –
then flew on falling into distance till
they broke across the local bush and
trees: it was a sight of bountiful
majesty and integrity: the having
patterns and routes, breaking
from them to explore other patterns or
better ways to routes, and then the
return: a dance sacred as the sap in
the trees, permanent in its descriptions
as the ripples round the brook's
ripplestone: fresh as this particular
flood of burn breaking across us now
from the sun.

40   A. R. AMMONS (1926–2001)

AT THE CEMETERY,
WALNUT GROVE PLANTATION,
SOUTH CAROLINA, 1989

among the rocks
at walnut grove
your silence drumming
in my bones,
tell me your names.

nobody mentioned slaves
and yet the curious tools
shine with your fingerprints.
nobody mentioned slaves
but somebody did this work
who had no guide, no stone,
who molders under rock.

tell me your names,
tell me your bashful names
and i will testify.

the inventory lists ten slaves
but only men were recognized.

among the rocks
at walnut grove

some of these honored dead
were dark
some of these dark
were slaves
some of these slaves
were women
some of them did this
honored work.
tell me your names
foremothers, brothers,
tell me your dishonored names.
here lies
here lies
here lies
here lies
hear

NIGHT FISHING

I bait my lines
with the scent of old planks
rotting over the Tuckasegee
River where drowsy snakes
coil in the rushes and lightning
bugs fizzle like spirits
of nightcrawlers nibbled
by minnows. No catch
in my throat but this aching
to wade into lazy black water
and stand all night long
in its leavetaking, calling
the fish home to Mama.

JANUARY DROUGHT

It needn't be tinder, this juncture of the year,
a cigarette second guessed from car to brush.

The woods' parchment is given
to cracking asunder the first puff of wind.
Yesterday a big sycamore came across First
and Hawthorne and is there yet.

The papers say it has to happen,
if just as dribs and drabs on the asbestos siding.
But tonight is buckets of stars as hard and dry
    as dimes.

A month's supper things stacks in the sink.
Tea brews from water stoppered in the bath
and any thirst carried forward is quenched
    thinking you,
piece by piece, an Xmas gift hidden
and found weeks after: the ribbon, the box.

I have reservoirs of want enough
to freeze many nights over.

DIORAMA

The Blue Hole Summer Fair, set up and spread out
like a butterfly pinned down on paper. Twin bright-lit
wings, identically shaped (and fenced) and sized.

This side holds the waffled-tin (and oven-hot) huts of
the Home Arts Booths and Contests, the hay-sweet
display-cages for the 4-H livestock, the streamer-hung
display-stages where girl-beauties twirl and try for
queen. There's rosette-luster (and -lusting), and the
marching band wearing a hole in Sousa. And (pursed)
gaggles and clutches of feather-white neighbor-
women, eyeballing us like we're pig's feet in a jar.
  I wonder does her boy talk Chinese?
          You ever seen that kind of black-headed?
                Blue shine all in it like a crow.

This other wing (the one I'm back-sneaking, side-
slipping, turnstiling into) dips and slopes down to
low-lying marsh-mire: whiffs of pluff-mud stink and
live gnat-pack poison, carnie-cots and -trailers camped
on ooze. They've got (rickety) rides, and tent-shows
with stains, and rackety bare-bulbed stalls of Hoop-La
Game (*RING-A-COKE!*) and Rebel Yell and Shoot
the Gook Down. Stand here, on this smutch-spot:
don't these mirrors show you strange?

45

Crowds are gathering. Yonder there and down, the
yolk-glow of a tent is drawing men on (and in) the way
a car-crash does, or a cockfight sure enough, or neon.
The ticket-boy's getting mobbed at the fly of the door.
  No sign in sight, except for the X of the Dixie-
    flag ironed across his t-shirt.
  I am bone-broke but falling into line.
  The men upwind of me are leaking chaw-spit
    and pennies.
  That, plus the eye-hunger spreading like a rumor
    through the swarm.
  The rib-skinny doorkeeper's hollering: *bet now,*
    bout's bout startin!
  Over his shoulder, a ropy yellow light.
  Also: circles of white tobacco-smoke, and
    bleacher-rows of (cooncalling) men who
    know my daddy.
  – And there he is, up in front with some tall man,
    iron-arming two black-chested boys toward
    the ring.

CRITTERS

If they have lived in a wood
It is a wood.
If they have lived on plains
It is grass rolling
Under their feet forever.

— JAMES DICKEY

THE MOCKING BIRD

Superb and sole, upon a plumëd spray
That o'er the general leafage boldly grew,
He summ'd the woods in song; or typic drew
The watch of hungry hawks, the lone dismay
Of languid doves when long their lovers stray,
And all birds' passion-plays that sprinkle dew
At morn in brake or bosky avenue.
Whate'er birds did or dreamed, this bird could say.
Then down he shot, bounced airily along
The sward, twitched in a grasshopper, made song
Midflight, perched, prinked, and to his art again.
Sweet Science, this large riddle read me plain:
How may the death of that dull insect be
The life of yon trim Shakespeare on the tree?

SIDNEY LANIER (1842–1881)   49

THE WHIPPOORWILL

Above lone woodland ways that led
To dells the stealthy twilights tread
The west was hot geranium red;
And still, and still,
Along old lanes the locusts sow
With clustered pearls the Maytimes know,
Deep in the crimson afterglow,
We heard the homeward cattle low,
And then the far-off, far-off woe
Of "whippoorwill!" of "whippoorwill!"

Beneath the idle beechen boughs
We heard the far bells of the cows
Come slowly jangling towards the house;
And still, and still,
Beyond the light that would not die
Out of the scarlet-haunted sky;
Beyond the evening-star's white eye
Of glittering chalcedony,
Drained out of dusk the plaintive cry
Of "whippoorwill," of "whippoorwill."

And in the city oft, when swims
The pale moon o'er the smoke that dims
Its disc, I dream of wildwood limbs;
And still, and still,
I seem to hear, where shadows grope
Mid ferns and flowers that dewdrops rope, –
Lost in faint deeps of heliotrope
Above the clover-sweetened slope, –
Retreat, despairing, past all hope,
The whippoorwill, the whippoorwill.

MADISON CAWEIN (1865–1914)

SOUTHERN GOTHIC
for W.E.B. & P.R.

Something of how the homing bee at dusk
Seems to inquire, perplexed, how there can be
No flowers here, not even withered stalks of flowers,
Conjures a garden where no garden is
And trellises too frail almost to bear
The memory of a rose, much less a rose.
Great oaks, more monumentally great oaks now
Than ever when the living rose was new,
Cast shade that is the more completely shade
Upon a house of broken windows merely
And empty nests up under broken eaves.
No damask any more prevents the moon,
But it unravels, peeling from a wall,
Red roses within roses within roses.

THE HEAVEN OF ANIMALS

Here they are. The soft eyes open.
If they have lived in a wood
It is a wood.
If they have lived on plains
It is grass rolling
Under their feet forever.

Having no souls, they have come,
Anyway, beyond their knowing.
Their instincts wholly bloom
And they rise.
The soft eyes open.

To match them, the landscape flowers,
Outdoing, desperately
Outdoing what is required:
The richest wood,
The deepest field.

For some of these,
It could not be the place
It is, without blood.
These hunt, as they have done,
But with claws and teeth grown perfect,

More deadly than they can believe.
They stalk more silently,
And crouch on the limbs of trees,
And their descent
Upon the bright backs of their prey

May take years
In a sovereign floating of joy.
And those that are hunted
Know this as their life,
Their reward: to walk

Under such trees in full knowledge
Of what is in glory above them,
And to feel no fear,
But acceptance, compliance.
Fulfilling themselves without pain

At the cycle's center,
They tremble, they walk
Under the tree,
They fall, they are torn,
They rise, they walk again.

RIDING LESSON

I learned two things
from an early riding teacher.
He held a nervous filly
in one hand and gestured
with the other, saying "Listen.
Keep one leg on one side,
the other leg on the other side,
and your mind in the middle."

He turned and mounted.
She took two steps, then left
the ground, I thought for good.
But she came down hard, humped
her back, swallowed her neck,
and threw her rider as you'd
throw a rock. He rose, brushed
his pants and caught his breath,
and said, "See that's the way
to do it. When you see
they're gonna throw you, get off."

HENRY TAYLOR (1942–)

TURKEY VULTURES

The red drill of their faces, pink-tipped,
grubbed in gore, cyclopean in their hunger
for the dead but not the dying, lugubrious
on their perches from towers, in trees, where they
convene like ushers on church steps.

Heads sculpted to fit cane handles, claws
to dibble seed, to sort out the warp of sinew
from the woof, unwind the gray bobbins of brain.
Assiduous as cats as they clean, wing scouring
wing, until the head polished like a gem

gleams, and the ears no more than lacy holes
are sieves for passing air or molecules of gas.
These birds, who wear the face of what will last,
congregating but not crowding, incurious
and almost patient with their dead.

ZERO HOUR

Bittern, hawk, and osprey tend
   in their private circles near
orders scrawled across the page,
though the willing victims send
postcards to another age
    gazing up in fear.

Alligators known to dwell
   in the analytic root
theorize about the will.
Frequently consigned to hell,
inconvenient villains still
    prepare to shoot.

Will indignant vultures perch,
    waiting for the halt and weak
on whose bounty they descend?
In a large and vacant church,
words whose meanings some defend
    have yet to speak.

FLOUNDER

Here, she said, *put this on your head.*
She handed me a hat.
You 'bout as white as your dad,
and you gone stay like that.

Aunt Sugar rolled her nylons down
around each bony ankle,
and I rolled down my white knee socks
letting my thin legs dangle,

circling them just above water
and silver backs of minnows
flitting here then there between
the sun spots and the shadows.

This is how you hold the pole
to cast the line out straight.
Now put that worm on your hook,
throw it out and wait.

She sat spitting tobacco juice
into a coffee cup.
Hunkered down when she felt the bite,
jerked the pole straight up

reeling and tugging hard at the fish
that wriggled and tried to fight back.
A flounder, she said, and *you can tell
'cause one of its sides is black.*

The other side is white, she said.
It landed with a thump.
I stood there watching that fish flip-flop,
switch sides with every jump.

VOLUNTEERS AND BLUEGRASS

POEMS OF TENNESSEE AND KENTUCKY

LITTLE GIFFEN

Out of the focal and foremost fire,
Out of the hospital walls as dire,
Smitten of grapeshot and gangrene,
(Eighteenth battle, and he sixteen!)
Spectre! Such as you seldom see,
Little Giffen, of Tennessee.

"Take him — and welcome!" the surgeons said;
"Little the doctor can help the dead!"
So we took him and brought him where
The balm was sweet in the summer air;
And we laid him down on a wholesome bed —
Utter Lazarus, heel to head!

And we watched the war with abated breath —
Skeleton boy against skeleton death.
Months of torture, how many such!
Weary weeks of the stick and crutch;
And still a glint of the steel-blue eye
Told of a spirit that wouldn't die.

And didn't. Nay, more! In death's despite
The crippled skeleton learned to write.
"Dear Mother," at first, of course; and then
"Dear Captain," inquiring about the men.

Captain's answer: "Of eighty-and-five,
Giffen and I are left alive."

Word of gloom from the war, one day;
"Johnston pressed at the front, they say."
Little Giffen was up and away;
A tear – his first – as he bade good-by,
Dimmed the glint of his steel-blue eye.
"I'll write, if spared!" There was news of the fight;
But none of Giffen. He did not write.

I sometimes fancy that, were I king
Of the princely knights of the Golden Ring,
With the song of the minstrel in mine ear,
And the tender legend that trembles here,
I'd give the best on his bended knee,
The whitest soul of my chivalry,
For Little Giffen, of Tennessee.

KNOXVILLE, TENNESSEE

I always like summer
best
you can eat fresh corn
from daddy's garden
and okra
and greens
and cabbage
and lots of
barbecue
and buttermilk and homemade ice-cream
at the church picnic
and listen to
gospel music
outside
at the church
homecoming
and go to the mountains with
your grandmother
and go barefooted
and be warm
all the time
not only when you go to bed
and sleep

NIKKI GIOVANNI (1943–)   65

AUDUBON DRIVE, MEMPHIS

There's a black-and-white photo of Elvis
and his father Vernon in their first swimming pool.
Elvis is about twenty-one and "Heartbreak Hotel"
has just sold a million.
When he bought the house,
mainly for his mother Gladys they say,
it didn't have a pool,
so this is new.
The water is up to the legs of Vernon's trunks
and rising slowly as he stands there
at attention almost.
Elvis is sitting or kneeling on the bottom,
water nearly to his shoulders,
his face as blank and white
as the five feet of empty poolside at his back.
The two of them are looking at the other side
of the pool and waiting for it to fill.
In the book somewhere
it says the water pump is broken.
The garden hose a cousin found is not in the frame,
but that's where the water is coming from.
In the background over Vernon's head you can see
about three stalks of corn
against white pickets in a small garden
I guess Gladys planted.

You could press a point and say that in the corn
and the fence, the invisible country
cousin and mother, the looks on Elvis' and Vernon's
faces, the partly filled pool, we can read
their lives together, the land
they came from, the homage they first thought
they owed the wealth beginning to accumulate,
the corny songs and films,
and that would be close but not quite central.
Closer than that is the lack
of anything waiting in the pool we'd be
prompted to call legend
if we didn't know otherwise.
They're simply son and father wondering if it's true
they don't have to drive a truck
tomorrow for a living.
But that's not it either.
What it reduces to is the fact that most of us
know more or less everything
that is happening to them
as though it were a critical text
embracing even us and our half-mawkish
geographies of two or three word obituaries:
in the case of Kennedy, for example, I was walking
across a quad in Oxford,

Mississippi; King's death too caught me in motion,
drifting through dogwood in the Shenandoah.
As for Elvis,
there were some of us parked outside a gas station
just over the bridge from Pawley's Island
with the radio on.
That's enough.
I know the differences.
But don't think they're outright.
The photo is 1034 Audubon Drive, Memphis,
and then it's Hollywood,
still waiting for the pool to fill.

SAD AND ALONE

Well, this is nothing new, nothing
to rattle the rafters in the noggin,

this moment of remembering
and its kissing cousin, the waking dream.

I wonder if I'll remember it?
I've had a vision of a woman

reclining underneath a tree:
she's about half-naked and little by little

I'm sprinkling her burial mounds
with grass. This is the kind of work

I like. It lets me remember, and so
I do. I remember the time I laid

my homemade banjo in the fire
and let it burn. There was nothing else

to burn and the house was cold;
the cigar box curled inside the flames.

But the burst of heat was over soon,
and once the little roar was done,

I could hear the raindrops plopping up
the buckets and kettles, scattered out

like little ponds around the room.
It was night and I was a boy, alone

and left to listen to that old music.
I liked it. I've liked it ever since.

I loved the helpless people I loved.
That's what a little boy will do,

but a grown man will turn it all
to sadness and let it soak his heart

until he wrings it out and dreams
about another kind of love,

some afternoon beneath a tree.
Burial mounds – that's hilarious.

JERRY LEE LEWIS PLAYS "THAT LUCKY OLD SUN" AT BAD BOB'S VAPORS CLUB, MEMPHIS, TENNESSEE

I'll tell it if you let me, my story of those nights we
     spent watching the Killer play
a smoky room down on Brooks Road, almost to State
     Line. Can't you hear the note
of reverence in my voice, the sweet pity of tragedy?
     Even when he wasn't half trying,
the songs fell from his lips so sorrow-encrusted and
     smoldering, so flavorful I'd swear
they'd been basketed from the roiling grease of a
     deep-fryer, his offhand rendering
of "That Lucky Old Sun" owing nothing to Ray
     Charles, and everything. *Show me*
that river . . . take me across. There was an inwardness to
     how he spoke the song, owning
the piece for just that moment, his leaning over to tell
     the microphone what he had to tell it
so personal an act we were almost shamed by our
     fascination. The song's a prayer,
another brief hymn to the emptiness inside us and
     what we hope might come
to fill it. On the piano a cigar was cocked and cold in
     the ashtray, waiting to be relit

when the song was done. Just a night of sight-seeing,
    September 1988, gone slumming
to hear the great and forgotten, none of us quite
    young enough to be young anymore.
The Vapors Club was exactly what you're imagining,
    show starts at ten, five dollar cover
at the door. The gray-blue light, where there was
    light, had grown so stale and clouded
it seemed to have clabbered, and even the shadows in
    the shadowy room were bowed
with the weight of something I didn't have a name for.
    The regulars bore it like soldiers –
paying customers flammable with hairspray and spent
    chances, slickened with a whiskey glow,
Ten High bourbon redistilled through their pores,
    sugary and volatile. Everyone in the place
had twenty years and a marriage or two on me.
    They'd lost something time took, the edges
of experience as fine and full of meaning as the
    cuttings in the grooves of an LP record
played too many times on a console stereo in the
    living room, a diamond stylus harrowing
its windy memory from the satiny grooves. I was just
    learning to love, tallying what cost
to lose myself as one long breath into another person,
    not knowing what would be left of me

once I was drawn back into myself. There is a point
    past which we will never again be able
to call ourselves detached, but on that night it was just
    music, a man punishing a piano
for wanting to keep something clenched in the tension
    of its iron harp, just a few hours
taking us toward another night's savory fatigue and
    upending, the insects' pulsed cries measuring
what was left of the year's heat, parking lot gravel
    crunching underfoot, then the car bounding
over the curb back onto Brooks Road, the bar smells
    we would wear for awhile, dance sweat
and menthol 100s, hair spray and Kiwi shoe polish,
    spray-on perfume. Then the driving
back to Midtown and our own shabby rooms, the car
    windows down, details of the skyline
edge-etched to the windshield, unheavened, sense-
    bound, all of us silent and rehearsing
our arrangement of the night's sharps and flats, a
    version shaped to suit our own dying voices.

BOBBY C. ROGERS (1964–)   73

WARTIME

In the black mirror
a woman's trying to erase names:
No, she's brushing a boy's hair.

— YUSEF KOMUNYAKAA

SHILOH
A Requiem (April, 1862)

Skimming lightly, wheeling still,
    The swallows fly low
Over the field in clouded days,
    The forest-field of Shiloh –
Over the field where April rain
Solaced the parched ones stretched in pain
Through the pause of night
That followed the Sunday fight
    Around the church of Shiloh –
The church so lone, the log-built one,
That echoed to many a parting groan
        And natural prayer
    Of dying foemen mingled there –
Foemen at morn, but friends at eve –
    Fame or country least their care:
(What like a bullet can undeceive!)
    But now they lie low,
While over them the swallows skim,
    And all is hushed at Shiloh.

HERMAN MELVILLE (1819–1891)

CHARLESTON

Calm as that second summer which precedes
    The first fall of the snow,
In the broad sunlight of heroic deeds,
    The City bides the foe.

As yet, behind their ramparts stern and proud,
    Her bolted thunders sleep –
Dark Sumter, like a battlemented cloud,
    Looms o'er the solemn deep.

No Calpe frowns from lofty cliff or scar
    To guard the holy strand;
But Moultrie holds in leash her dogs of war
    Above the level sand.

And down the dunes a thousand guns lie couched,
    Unseen, beside the flood –
Like tigers in some Orient jungle crouched
    That wait and watch for blood.

Meanwhile, through streets still echoing with trade,
    Walk grave and thoughtful men,
Whose hands may one day wield the patriot's blade
    As lightly as the pen.

And maidens, with such eyes as would grow dim
    Over a bleeding hound,

Seem each one to have caught the strength of him
      Whose sword she sadly bound.

Thus girt without and garrisoned at home,
      Day patient following day,
Old Charleston looks from roof, and spire, and dome,
      Across her tranquil bay.

Ships, through a hundred foes, from Saxon lands
      And spicy Indian ports,
Bring Saxon steel and iron to her hands,
      And summer to her courts.

But still, along yon dim Atlantic line,
      The only hostile smoke
Creeps like a harmless mist above the brine,
      From some frail, floating oak.

Shall the spring dawn, and she still clad in smiles,
      And with an unscathed brow,
Rest in the strong arms of her palm-crowned isles,
      As fair and free as now?

We know not; in the temple of the Fates
      God has inscribed her doom;
And, all untroubled in her faith, she waits
      The triumph or the tomb.

HENRY TIMROD (1828–1867)

"UNDER THE SHADE OF THE TREES"

What are the thoughts that are stirring his breast?
   What is the mystical vision he sees?
– "Let us pass over the river, and rest
   Under the shade of the trees."

Has he grown sick of his toils and his tasks?
   Sighs the worn spirit for respite or ease?
Is it a moment's cool halt that he asks
   Under the shade of the trees?

Is it the gurgle of waters whose flow
   Ofttimes has come to him, borne on the breeze,
Memory listens to, lapsing so low,
   Under the shade of the trees?

Nay – though the rasp of the flesh was so sore,
   Faith, that had yearnings far keener than these,
Saw the soft sheen of the Thitherward Shore
   Under the shade of the trees; –

Caught the high psalms of ecstatic delight –
   Heard the harps harping, like soundings of seas –
Watched earth's assoiled ones walking in white
   Under the shade of the trees.

Oh, was it strange he should pine for release,
    Touched to the soul with such transports as these, –
He who so needed the balsam of peace,
    Under the shade of the trees?

Yea, it was noblest for him – it was best
    (Questioning naught of our Father's decrees),
There to pass over the river and rest
    Under the shade of the trees!

HUNTING CIVIL WAR RELICS
AT NIMBLEWILL CREEK

As he moves the mine detector
A few inches over the ground,
Making it vitally float
Among the ferns and weeds,
I come into this war
Slowly, with my one brother,
Watching his face grow deep
Between the earphones,
For I can tell
If we enter the buried battle
Of Nimblewill
Only by his expression.

Softly he wanders, parting
The grass with a dreaming hand.
No dead cry yet takes root
In his clapped ears
Or can be seen in his smile.
But underfoot I feel
The dead regroup,
The burst metals all in place,
The battle lines be drawn
Anew to include us
In Nimblewill,
And I carry the shovel and pick

More as if they were
Bright weapons that I bore.
A bird's cry breaks
In two, and into three parts.
We cross the creek; the cry
Shifts into another,
Nearer, bird, and is
Like the shout of a shadow —
Lived-with, appallingly close —
Or the soul, pronouncing
"Nimblewill":
Three tones; your being changes.

We climb the bank;
A faint light glows
On my brother's mouth.
I listen, as two birds fight
For a single voice, but he
Must be hearing the grave,
In pieces, all singing
To his clamped head,
For he smiles as if
He rose from the dead within
Green Nimblewill
And stood in his grandson's shape.

No shot from the buried war
Shall kill me now,
For the dead have waited here
A hundred years to create
Only the look on the face
Of my one brother,
Who stands among them, offering
A metal dish
Afloat in the trembling weeds,
With a long-buried light on his lips
At Nimblewill
And the dead outsinging two birds.

I choke the handle
Of the pick, and fall to my knees
To dig wherever he points,
To bring up mess tin or bullet,
To go underground
Still singing, myself,
Without a sound,
Like a man who renounces war,
Or one who shall lift up the past,
Not breathing "Father,"
At Nimblewill,
But saying, "Fathers! Fathers!"

MY OWN LITTLE CIVIL WAR

I come from the only county in Tennessee that did
    not secede
Throughout the entire Civil War,
                Sullivan County,
Rock-ribbed, recalcitrant, Appalachian cornerstone.
My kinfolk were otherwise,
Arkansans and Mississippians,
                Virginians and Tarheels.
Still, I was born just a half mile from Shiloh
    churchyard,
And had a relative, the family story goes, who
    served there,
Confederate quartermaster,
             who took the occasion, that first day,
To liberate many bills
From Union coffers as the Johnnys swept through
    to the river,
And never replaced them when the Bluebellies
    swept back
And through the following afternoon.

My great-grandfather Wright left VMI to join up
With Lee and the Army of Northern Virginia
Somewhere near Richmond,
            and ended up,

Lucky lad, a staff officer in the general's command.
Who knows how many letters that took?
After the war he went back to Lexington, with Lee,
The general to Washington College and immortality,
Capt. Wright at the far end of town,
                              still marching away the lost cause.
Marse Robert has his horse and white tomb
Under the oak trees.
My great-grandfather has his name in a long thin line
Of others who were captains of the Corps of Cadets,
                              too little, boys, too late.

My great-grandfather Penzel, four years in the
         country,
Saddled up in 1861 in Little Rock
With the Capital City Guards
                              and struck out for Tennessee.
His name is last on the list, carved in print on an
         obelisk,
In front of a civic building somewhere near
         downtown.
Like just about everyone else, he finished the war as
         a captain,
Enduring the raw campaigns
                              of southeast Tennessee,
Chickamauga, two years in Rock Island prison, deep
Wounds in his mouth and elsewhere,

Then back, like all the others, into the thick of it.
A long way for a country boy,
                                        slaveless, and no stake in it,
From the green hills of Bohemia.

There are letters from Isaac Wright,
                                Bladen County, North Carolina,
1856,
To his son near Lafayette Courthouse, Red River,
    Arkansas,
A dozen or so, I cannot decipher.
                                Political
And familial, about President Franklin Pierce,
Wishing that John C. Calhoun
                                were still alive and president
Instead, and the Constitutional rights of the South
Established with greater force,
                                and greater clarity.
"I fear that we shall yet have difficulties with our
    Northern Brethren."
And then the price of negroes,
Nearby farms, the fear of high water,
            the price of cotton, always the price of cotton.
The "love to Elizabeth, my son, and you and the
    children."

All this from the documents
                              left by my great-aunt Marcella,
A folder that also holds,
Inexplicably, my grandmother's marriage license
And one short sketch, so titled, of the Fulton and
        Nowland families.
So much for all that . . .
                              However, wrapped in wax paper,
Among the letters, is another small envelope
Containing a lock, so called,
                              of Robert E. Lee's hair,
Sent by him to the wife of the lucky lad from VMI . . .

That's it, my own little Civil War –
                              a lock of hair,
A dozen unreadable letters,
A obit or two,
And half the weight and half-life
                    of a half-healed and hurting world.

ELEGY FOR THE NATIVE GUARDS

> *Now that the salt of their blood*
> *Stiffens the saltier oblivion of the sea . . .*
>   — ALLEN TATE

We leave Gulfport at noon; gulls overhead
trailing the boat – streamers, noisy fanfare –
all the way to Ship Island. What we see
first is the fort, its roof of grass, a lee –
half reminder of the men who served there –
a weathered monument to some of the dead.

Inside we follow the ranger, hurried
though we are to get to the beach. He tells
of graves lost in the Gulf, the island split
in half when Hurricane Camille hit,
shows us casemates, cannons, the store that sells
souvenirs, tokens of history long buried.

The Daughters of the Confederacy
has placed a plaque here, at the fort's entrance –
each Confederate soldier's name raised hard
in bronze; no names carved for the Native Guards –
2nd Regiment, Union men, black phalanx.
What is monument to their legacy?

All the grave markers, all the crude headstones –
water-lost. Now fish dart among their bones,
and we listen for what the waves intone.
Only the fort remains, near forty feet high,
round, unfinished, half open to the sky,
the elements – wind, rain – God's deliberate eye.

BAYOU AND THE LONE STAR

POEMS OF LOUISIANA AND TEXAS

I SAW IN LOUISIANA A LIVE-OAK GROWING

I saw in Louisiana a live-oak growing,
All alone stood it and the moss hung down from the
    branches,
Without any companion it grew there uttering joyous
    leaves of dark green,
And its look, rude, unbending, lusty, made me think of
    myself,
But I wonder'd how it could utter joyous leaves
    standing alone there without its friend near, for
    I knew I could not,
And I broke off a twig with a certain number of leaves
    upon it, and twined around it a little moss,
And brought it away, and I have placed it in sight in
    my room,
It is not needed to remind me as of my own dear
    friends,
(For I believe lately I think of little else than of them,)
Yet it remains to me a curious token, it makes me
    think of manly love;
For all that, and though the live-oak glistens there in
    Louisiana solitary in a wide flat space,
Uttering joyous leaves all its life without a friend a
    lover near,
I know very well I could not.

WALT WHITMAN (1819–1892)   93

DRYCLEANERS

At the drycleaners I stand in line, my feet
shuffling weight from side to side,
impatience all over me while the woman,
light brown, with her Creole story drones on.
In New Orleans none would notice.
She's exotic in Baltimore, a dawn bird
everything hears. Even the clerk
leans into her tale, clucking softly. When
people behind me cough, she won't be
rushed. She's got her whole story to go.
Soon there's a man she never married,
her mother opposed, far away still, and he
went into a bar, wrong place, wrong color,
wrong words, maybe, a good man.
He'll never come away of there, not comin'
home, geraniums on the back porch,
and not replace the bad tire her Honda has,
who could always be telling her what time
does in the kitchen if she stand half
naked letting his dog go on out. So
let me pay you for him, give you money
because you is nice and I remember,
her nearly singing voice sighs. The sleeved
pants, two shirts hang on the brass ring, all
finished, unclaimed, the stiffened

stains gone away. The perfectly starched
cloth a redemption so beautiful
it might be the linen of royalty, but small
for a man two of us will think of as
sleep scuffs house walls like tide under a boat.
How nice they are, these women doing
the little one person can for another
which is, in the end, a wash
of memorable words that leave you standing.

DAVE SMITH (1942–) 95

FAT TUESDAY

I'll lick these screwfaced torches all night long
and chew the beads and blue doubloons that sail
from iron balconies mossy in the dark,
I'll walk down Royal Street dressed as a sweetgum tree
pretending my back is front, big whiskeybreath for all
who love this season of preparing. I'll be ready
for denial, to put away all fat things, all spoils,
the meat and bulky jewels of wanting
anything, even the wish to want.
The King salutes us from his golden dragon.
He is our food today. Eat his bones, his furs,
his crown and sceptre. Eat his fat throne and flesh,
his voice that laughs us into easy forgiveness.
I'll eat the King and break his will inside me
and toward tomorrow mix him with my swallowed
pearls and coins and whiskey and days.

GOING FOR PEACHES,
FREDERICKSBURG, TEXAS

Those with experience look for a special kind.
Red globe, the skin slips off like a fine silk camisole.
Boy breaks one open with his hands. Yes, it's good,
my old relatives say, but we'll look around.
They want me to stop at every peach stand
between Stonewall and Fredericksburg,
leave the air conditioner running,
jump out and ask the price.

Coming up here they talked about
the best ways to die. One favors a plane crash,
but not over a city. The other wants to make sure
her grass is watered when she goes.
Ladies, ladies! This peach is fine,
it blushes on both sides.
But they want to keep driving.

In Fredericksburg the houses are stone,
they remind me of wristwatches, glass polished,
years ticking by in each wall.
I don't like stone, says one. What if it fell?
I don't like Fredericksburg, says the other.
Too many Germans driving too slow.
She herself is German as Stuttgart.
The day presses forward, wearing complaints
like charms on its bony wrist.

Actually ladies (I can't resist),
I don't think you wanted peaches after all,
you just wanted a nip of scenery,
some hills to tuck behind your head.
The buying starts immediately, from a scarfed woman
    who says
I gave up teachin' for peachin'.
She has us sign the guest book.
One aunt insists on re-loading into her own box,
so she can see the fruit on the bottom.
One rejects any slight bruise.
But Ma'am, the seller insists, nature isn't perfect.
Her hands are spotted, like a peach.

On the road, cars weave loose patterns between lanes.
We will float in flowery peach-smell
back to our separate kettles, our private tables
    and knives,
and line up the bounty,
deciding which ones go where.
A canned peach, says one aunt, lasts ten years.
She was 87 last week. But a frozen peach
tastes better on ice cream.
Everything we have learned so far,
the stages of ripening alive in our skins,
on a day that was real to us, that was summer,
motion going out and memory coming in.

THE SINGERS

1

You lift a piece of meat to your mouth
with the silver fork
you took from the burning house.
It glitters in your hand,
a sliver of light on mud.
Don't leave me, woman, not now.
I smell the shit odor of fear again
like the night five years ago
when I crossed the Rio Grande into Texas.
The Carranzistas had killed Zapata
and they'd kill me too, if I stayed in Chihuahua.
But half a mile in, I saw him:
Zapata on the ground in front of me.
He bowed and danced slowly around his sombrero,
and the bullet holes in his body,
black, eight-pointed stars,
gave off a luminous darkness.

Back in Mexico, I don't remember riding,
only standing beside my horse
outside a whitewashed house.
When I looked through the window,
I saw you and your father, Indian, like me,
sitting at a table, bare, except for a silver fork.

Help me, I said. *I rode with Zapata.*
But neither of you moved.
You started singing: *Zapata, Zapata, your blood is so red.*
Zapata, Zapata, you're dead.
Who's at the window, a ghost, a ghost, only a ghost.
And when I lifted my hands,
they were transparent,
my bones, colorless light.
I struck the window,
they shattered
and I smelled fear again. I could see it:
the black outline of a horse on its hind legs,
a zero burning on its belly,
burning for me, Rosebud Morales.
I screamed, screamed my name
until I came back to myself
and could see my hands, their russet skin,
wrapping some straw in a ball.
I set it afire and threw it into the house.
When you ran out, I grabbed you.
You stabbed me with the fork, but I held on.
You kept singing while your father burned.

2

You wrap the Spanish Bible you can't read
in your shawl,
then you start running.
But I catch you by your braids,
drag you to the cooking fire and push your head in it.
When I let go, you stagger up
wearing a halo of flames.
Come on, sing with me: *Zapata, Zapata, your blood
     is so red.*
Sing, goddamnit. You fall.
The shadow of a train rises from your body
and lightning zigzags from the smokestack.
The smokestack is a man. Zapata. I raise my pistol.
I'm not afraid of any sonofabitch on two feet.
I fire, then jam the barrel in my mouth.
Not even you, motherfucker, not even you.

YOU BRING OUT THE MEXICAN IN ME

You bring out the Mexican in me.
The hunkered thick dark spiral.
The core of a heart howl.
The bitter bile.
The tequila *lagrímas* on Saturday all
through next weekend Sunday.
You are the one I'd let go the other loves for,
surrender my one-woman house.
Allow you red wine in bed,
even with my vintage lace linens.
Maybe. Maybe.

For you.

You bring out the Dolores del Río in me.
The Mexican spitfire in me.
The raw *navajas*, glint and passion in me.
The raise Cain and dance with the rooster-footed
     devil in me.
The spangled sequin in me.
The eagle and serpent in me.
The *mariachi* trumpets of the blood in me.
The Aztec love of war in me.
The fierce obsidian of the tongue in me.
The *berrinchuda*, *bien-cabrona* in me.
The Pandora's curiosity in me.

The pre-Columbian death and destruction in me.
The rainforest disaster, nuclear threat in me.
The fear of fascists in me.
Yes, you do. Yes, you do.

You bring out the colonizer in me.
The holocaust of desire in me.
The Mexico City '85 earthquake in me.
The Popocatepetl/Ixtaccíhuatl in me.
The tidal wave of recession in me.
The Agustín Lara hopeless romantic in me.
The *barbacoa taquitos* on Sunday in me.
The cover the mirrors with cloth in me.

Sweet twin. My wicked other,
I am the memory that circles your bed nights,
that tugs you taut as moon tugs ocean.
I claim you all mine,
arrogant as Manifest Destiny.
I want to rattle and rent you in two.
I want to defile you and raise hell.
I want to pull out the kitchen knives,
dull and sharp, and whisk the air with crosses.
Me sacas lo mexicana en mi,
like it or not, honey.

You bring out the Uled-Nayl in me.
The stand-back-white-bitch in me.
The switchblade in the boot in me.
The Acapulco cliff diver in me.
The *Flecha Roja* mountain disaster in me.
The *dengue* fever in me.
The *¡Alarma!* murderess in me.
I could kill in the name of you and think
it worth it. Brandish a fork and terrorize rivals,
female and male, who loiter and look at you,
languid in your light. Oh,

I am evil. I am the filth goddess Tlazoltéotl.
I am the swallower of sins.
The lust goddess without guilt.
The delicious debauchery. You bring out
the primordial exquisiteness in me.
The nasty obsession in me.
The corporal and venial sin in me.
The original transgression in me.

Red ocher. Yellow ocher. Indigo. Cochineal.
Piñón. Copal. Sweetgrass. Myrrh.
All you saints, blessed and terrible,
Virgen de Guadalupe, diosa Coatlicue,
I invoke you.

Quiero ser tuya. Only yours. Only you.
Quiero amarte. Atarte. Amarrarte.
Love the way a Mexican woman loves. Let
me show you. Love the only way I know how.

RATTLESNAKES HAMMERED
ON THE WALL

Seven of them pinned in blood by
long, shiny tails, three of them still

alive and writhing against the wood,
their heaviness whipping the wall

as they try to break free,
rattles beating in unison,

hisses slowly dying in silence,
the other four hanging stiff

like ropes to another life,
patterns of torn skin dripping

with power and loss, the wonder
of who might have done this

turning in shock as all seven
suddenly come alive when

I get closer, pink mouths
trembling with white fangs,

lunging at me then falling back,
entangled in one another to form

twisted letters that spell a bloody
word I can't understand.

VIRGIN MULE

The conversations of the French
Quarter mules in their stables
after a full day of pulling
tourists and voters over cobble-
stones is not espresso witty
and in their dark no TVs feed
them news of the ends of mules
elsewhere in the Middle East
and West. In our stables the ends
of others are a fact of atmosphere.
The yoyos on the mystery island
nextdoor are revving familiar tools
in backyard now gripped by failure
first of electricity than of
a meaner something that'll grow
into nothing we'll know in the A.M.
Once they were visitors like us
then they grew mulish in their
bubbles and pulled whatever
was put around their necks in-
cluding a banner that said, About
What Kills Us We Know Little.
On certain nights after a good
internal fight we hear the voice-
less others through the glass

fearfully sweet'n'soft like dough.
Oh let the monsters in. Help us
rise above our not seeing them,
may they let us into their eyes
as well. Banish the blindness
of these cobblestones, clop, clop.
But! Pffsst! Our notes are in-
complete. Loving you was
never on the agenda. Better
to sing as roughly as the stones.
On Memorial Day we had one
thousand hotdogs & counting.
Didn't visit a single graveyard.
We the Grant Wood folks scan
the sky for incoming missiles:
blips ourselves we understand
timing and touring in America.
The gilded dads in the portraits
sought the idealized continuity
now moving before us democratically
in showers of pixels and dots.
I'll go with the distracted mariner,
my lover, and we'll be in the world.
It will be late by then and dark.
We lyric virgin mules keep our
book of hours in a dream apart,
having stranded a billion turistas.

But we could not break the chummy hand.
Ready to brave the snow without a hat,
severe weather notwithstanding,
we merely nod and understand.

IMMOLATUS

She had her feet in the trough,
Nosing into the golden corn,
When daddy did a half spin
& brought down the sledgehammer.
She sank to the mud.
An oak branch bowed
As they tightened the rope
To a creaky song of pulley wheels.
A few leaves left
For the wind to whip down,
They splashed hot water
& shaved her with blades
That weighed less each year.
Snow geese honked overhead
& Sirius balanced on a knifetip.
Wintertime bit into the ropy guts
Falling into a number-3 tub
That emptied out in a gray gush
Like the end of a ditch
Choked with slime & roses.
Something love couldn't make
Walk again. I had a boy's job
Lugging water from the pump
& filling the iron washpot.
I threw pine knots on the blaze.

Soon her naked whiteness
Was a silence to split
Between
helpers & owner.
Liver, heart, & head
Flung to a foot tub.
They smiled as she passed
Through their hands. Next day
I tracked blood in a circle
Across dead grass, while fat
Boiled down to lye soap.

HOUSTON, 6 P.M.

Europe already sleeps beneath a coarse plaid of borders
and ancient hatreds: France nestled
up to Germany, Bosnia in Serbia's arms,
lonely Sicily in azure seas.

It's early evening here, the lamp is lit
and the dark sun swiftly fades.
I'm alone, I read a little, think a little,
listen to a little music.

I'm where there's friendship,
but no friends, where enchantment
grows without magic,
where the dead laugh.

I'm alone because Europe is sleeping. My love
sleeps in a tall house on the outskirts of Paris.
In Krakow and Paris my friends
wade in the same river of oblivion.

I read and think; in one poem
I found the phrase "There are blows so terrible . . .
Don't ask!" I don't. A helicopter
breaks the evening quiet.

Poetry calls us to a higher life,
but what's low is just as eloquent,
more plangent than Indo-European,
stronger than my books and records.

There are no nightingales or blackbirds here
with their sad, sweet cantilenas,
only the mockingbird who imitates
and mimics every living voice.

Poetry summons us to life, to courage
in the face of the growing shadow.
Can you gaze calmly at the Earth
like the perfect astronaut?

Out of harmless indolence, the Greece of books,
and the Jerusalem of memory there suddenly appears
the island of a poem, unpeopled;
some new Cook will discover it one day.

Europe is already sleeping. Night's animals,
mournful and rapacious,
move in for the kill.
Soon America will be sleeping, too.

ADAM ZAGAJEWSKI (1945–)   113

TO SYLVESTER FROM TERMINAL B

George H. W. Bush Airport, Houston, Texas

Dear Phil —
      I have always loved this terminal —
Even as a boy I roamed its lunar-lander halls,
And I never got over my happiness
With the crazy story of jet travel,
Never misunderstood how, from East Texas,
No one ever sees the ocean, nor honestly misses
Not seeing the ocean, what with the way our
      heat rises
In waves over the asphalt neighborhoods
                       and half-irrational trees,
What with the way our 254 counties
Seem always to have a whiff of uncertainty
Hanging above them, a sway
Of star-glitter that is part shine and part phewy,
And the way, too, I can't help but stroll
Inside these curvaceous hallways
Pleased as a poet among the daffodils!
And how every time I pass through this city,
I can't help but remember, too, that night
Outside Ruggles in Montrose —
One brother and I took to the parking lot after
      the beignets,

114

And he taught me "Leaving on a Jet Plane,"
                          two squeakers in the throes
Of a bad song that has a good heart.
                          You know,
I'm leaving on a jet plane. Don't know
When I'll be back again. Oh, babe, I hate to go.
What was my brother saying to me back then,
                          when neither of us had grown
Into manhood, when in that moment we could almost
    believe
Something was waiting for us in the future
Beyond the boom–chica-chica melodies of our
    Tex-Mex city
Where only in the burrito sheds could you find
    someone
To speak of war who might know that there is little
    difference
Between dying for your country and killing for your
    country?
Phil, any age is just so new.
                          I'll tell you this:
What's new in Terminal B is the 8-foot-tall bronze
    sculpture
Of the 41st President of the United States
Who adopted oily Midland and did OK, sure,

And whose second son you already know, your
        roommate
During the dire year you went to Phillips Academy –
The future governor of Florida, your homey!
Like everyone else in Terminal B,
The 41st President of the United States is in an
        8-foot-tall hurry.
He's windswept with the winds of change,
His tie blowing heroically over the left shoulder,
His jacket held vibrantly over the other shoulder,
A hustling bronze man
Hustling into a lone wind, some book in hand, too,
And his face taut with an unscoured vision –
                            an 8-foot-tall bronze saint
Is what you're supposed to feel when you stare up at
        his great
Great greatness! Something in the mind
Splits in half in moments like that,
As if one part of the brain cannot find the
        other part,
And Part A does not miss Part B,
And the contexts of humanity are lost
And what are to be found in the details are details,
And what are to be made from the details are also
        details.
Phil, I wish that statue had been dedicated to the
        Almighty

As a kind of slithery baptism wrestled out of a
      wildcatter.
Or, say, the 8-foot-tall bronze president is headed to
      the Bacchanalia!
With dancing maidens and cafés opened until eternity!
And the cathedrals straight as swords!
And every murmur comprehended by every stone!
And yet, when you look around Terminal B,
You see, for all the world, that everyone must come
      home to die.
I wonder: Is it the cloud-thick sky they need?
The white air that tightens over the decaying bodies?
Here's what my Houstonians need to know
About the man inside the statue:
On the evening of his defeat in 1992,
Somewhere past midnight, he wrote in his diary
That defeat "hurt, hurt, hurt. . . ." Then –
    Comfort the ones I've hurt and let down.
    Finish with a smile and some gusto.
– Phil, not long after that night of singing,
My brother and I tried to plant a garden
In the fenced-in backyard on Loch Lomond Drive
About forty-five miles from here,
And very little grew for a couple of Yiddish farmers
                    aged four and nine.
It was as if we were trying to plant our own names
Into the Texas earth

With the summer months humid
Even inside the tines of the rakes.
I guess we wanted to grow something
                          so as to carry our work
Into whatever travels lay ahead, whatever worries
Were to come along, come and go.
We furrowed, we dug, we seeded, we waited,
                          and sometimes watered –
Spinach bolted. Tomatoes cracked. And the
    cucumbers.
And the days went by with a wind we should have
    called *forbid*,
And the years went by with a wind we didn't call
    anything.
What can I say? What can I say?
We were nameless boys
Flowing straight up for years and then straight
    down –
And, in one city after another,
In phases of wandering into and out of lives,
We went in search of other brothers,
And we found them, too, from time to time,
And we added their singing to ours.
Sometimes, Phil, when the sun dims,
Taking nothing and giving nothing,
When the sun dims in a southwestern sky
Like this one, in August, in the unremodeled airport

              with its Moon Shot décor,
The sterile blossoms of a brotherly garden
Unfold in portraits of passing faces,
Men and women of every consequence,
As if they are chalked and erased with charcoal –
And they unfold inside distant brothers, too,
And in parents, and then parents that die.
Even when we expect death to come,
We are not ready when it does –
No, we are not ready, as we are seldom ready
When the sun etches out of the sky,
And the weeds we have not picked purr higher.
And the ocean two-thousand-five-hundred miles
      from here
Survives in its embers,
The ocean calling in the believers
With their fists thrust at the stars,
Their knuckles like honeycombs,
The believers straggling into the low waves,
And the sun-stunned winds blowing every which way.
           Phil, the Romans say, in wine there is truth.
OK then, I'm for wine!
               Especially here
In Bubba's Bar and Grill inside Terminal B!
Here, the podunks and bumbershoots,
The abdicators and the yiddle men
All get to have their say.

What I hear now is a lady with a two-step drawl
Calling my flight!
Look, I'll be leaving soon.
Even with all the brothers I've added,
I'm still missing one – gone out to find the wind
And we don't know when he's coming back.
That's not fate, that's the Book of Life's child
                                    singing in silence.
I write to hear, you draw to hear, a brother prays
      to hear.
But once – I almost heard that other brother!
And then I almost understood
How chance bleeds into the earth.
There's more to say, Phil, but the lady is calling
      my flight.
Sometimes it just feels bitter saying goodbye
      so often.
A few army recruits are loitering in the bookstalls.
Brothers of somebody.
                        We cannot save them, Phil,
Not with poetry, not with art,
                  nor with the songs of boys
                  nor the prayers of men.
One dies, another is born,
And the wreck of the heart unwrongs those we love.
We live in a world of matter and creatures
                        and unmemorized power.

Just boys, Phil.
Sometimes with the wind at their backs,
Other times a wind in their faces.
Just boys, passing through home.

THE ANIMAL INTELLIGENCES

Scrawling out my name in triplicate,
I can see this dread – the frigid rightness
of this claim form on the mahogany table –
as a family sickness. Immense worry
fixed the jawbone in my father's face,
hardening his eyes as he bore down
signing things, his shirt sleeves rolled up tightly,
the kitchen hazed by the thick cigarette smoke
of those hushed nights. I could say great pressure
crushed us early.
                    But in truth,
under the full weight of his watching,
I was delivered, summers, to my grandfather's
dryland farm. I was allowed to crouch
among the hay bales stacked in abandoned houses,
feeling the wood floors splitting under me,
touched in angular places where the sun
broke in, where black wasps lighted up
and darkened in their labors.
                              In truth
I remember squinting awestruck with an air gun
at my eye, firing until a trapped skunk
finished writing. Then running for the fence
with my brother, swooning in the smell,
over the cattle guard, down the sandy road,

into a skunkless field of vines.
And huddling there, breaking open
a black diamond melon, streaked with juice,
eating the heartmeat, both of us caked
brow to ankle with the indelible
flatland clay.
                    There are ways
that circumstance will choke a life to fit
these blank-lined pages, but I have been allowed,
at two years old, to take my grandfather's huge
straw hat in my hands, and put my whole face
into it, as if into plenitude myself,
smelling the sweat and diesel as he rested,
his chest heaving slowly, his face
soft and dark as loam.
                        Plowed earth,
the pungent aftermath, my white hand
holds the pen against the form and will not
finish it. Somewhere a man gets up
from his desk of obligations, his face
constricted from the lampglare. He wades out
shoulder-deep in his rows of corn stalks,
lighting up eyes and blurred hind legs,
and turns the flashlight off. He lets a breeze
wave all those nightblack leaves toward him

until the blindness in his mind dies out
and he hears the animal intelligences returning,
gnawing on stalks, burrowing nervously
to the source of the growing, frozen a moment
as a wave of dread blows over them,
then nosing back down to their labor, quietly
elated in the loam-rich fields of pay.

ODE TO BOUDIN

You are the chewing gum
of God. You are the reason
I know that skin
is only that, holds
more than it meets.
The heart of you is something
I don't quite get
but don't want to. Even
a fool like me can see
your broken
beauty, the way
out in this world where most
things disappear, driven
into ground, you are ground
already, & like rice
you rise. Drunken deacon,
sausage's half-brother,
jambalaya's baby mama,
you bring me back
to the beginning, to where things live
again. Homemade saviour,
you fed me the day
my father sat under flowers
white as the gloves of pallbearers
tossed on his bier.

Soon, hands will lower him
into ground richer
than even you.
For now, root of all
remembrance, your thick chain
sets me spinning, thinking
of how, like the small,
perfect, possible, silent soul
you spill out
like music, my daddy
dead, or grief,
or both – afterward his sisters
my aunts dancing
in the yard to a car radio
tuned to zydeco
beneath the pecan trees.

SINCE THE CITY TURNED BLUE

Down in New Orleans
for another church retreat
gone to hell with a night's drunken cheat.
I wake sick, pull out my rod, walk to the levee,
hook on a shrimp, cast and fall asleep.
Stirring between the stained grass and garbage,
horns, hammers and concrete resurrection –
somebody shouts
and I'm up fumbling, reeling, rod bent around the
     hazy sum
of a wild fish on a silvery run –
It's a devil, I yell,
lifting the deep-bodied, grunting swish
up to the group of orange vested apostles.
Ain't no devil, says a guy from the crew –
*Just a gaspergoo. Get 'em all the time
since the city's turned blue.*

HENRY HUGHES (1965–)

A CLOUD OF
WITNESSES

*get your own sound then notes go with your sound —
it's like a color, my color — I'm black brown with a
little red-orange in my skin*

— C. D. WRIGHT

A BALLAD OF TREES AND THE MASTER

Into the woods my Master went,
Clean forspent, forspent.
Into the woods my Master came,
Forspent with love and shame.
But the olives they were not blind to Him;
The little gray leaves were kind to Him:
The thorn-tree had a mind to Him
When into the woods He came.

Out of the woods my Master went,
And He was well content.
Out of the woods my Master came,
Content with death and shame.
When Death and Shame would woo Him last,
From under the trees they drew Him last:
'Twas on a tree they slew Him – last,
When out of the woods He came.

SIDNEY LANIER (1842–1881)   131

SYMPATHY

I know what the caged bird feels, alas!
　　When the sun is bright on the upland slopes;
When the wind stirs soft through the springing grass,
And the river flows like a stream of glass;
　　When the first bird sings and the first bud opes,
And the faint perfume from its chalice steals –
I know what the caged bird feels!

I know why the caged bird beats his wing
　　Till its blood is red on the cruel bars;
For he must fly back to his perch and cling
When he fain would be on the bough a-swing;
　　And a pain still throbs in the old, old scars
And they pulse again with a keener sting –
I know why he beats his wing!

I know why the caged bird sings, ah me,
　　When his wing is bruised and his bosom sore, –
When he beats his bars and he would be free;
It is not a carol of joy or glee,
　　But a prayer that he sends from his heart's deep
　　　　core,
But a plea, that upward to Heaven he flings –
I know why the caged bird sings!

132　PAUL LAURENCE DUNBAR (1872–1906)

SONNET: TO SILENCE

There are some qualities – some incorporate things,
    That have a double life, which thus is made
A type of that twin entity which springs
    From matter and light, evinced in solid and shade.
There is a two-fold *Silence* – sea and shore –
    Body and soul. One dwells in lonely places,
    Newly with grass o'ergrown; some solemn graces,
Some human memories and tearful lore,
Render him terrorless: his name's "No More."
He is the corporate Silence: dread him not!
    No power hath he of evil in himself;
But should some urgent fate (untimely lot!)
    Bring thee to meet his shadow (nameless elf,
That haunteth the dim regions where hath trod
No foot of man,) commend thyself to God!

EDGAR ALLAN POE (1809–1849)   133

FOUNDING FATHERS, NINETEENTH-CENTURY STYLE, SOUTHEAST U.S.A.

They were human, they suffered, wore long black coat
    and gold watch chain.
They stare from daguerreotype with severe
    reprehension,
Or from genuine oil, and you'd never guess any pain
In those merciless eyes that now remark our own
    time's sad declension.

Some composed declarations, remembering Jefferson's
    language.
Knew pose of the patriot, left hand in crook of the
    spine or
With finger to table, while right invokes the Lord's
    just rage.
There was always a grandpa, or cousin at least, who
    had been, of course, a real Signer.

Some were given to study, read Greek in the forest,
    and these
Longed for an epic to do their own deeds right honor;
Were Nestor by pigpen, in some tavern brawl played
    Achilles.
In the ring of Sam Houston they found, when he died,
    one word engraved: *Honor.*

Their children were broadcast, like millet seed flung
    in a wind-flare.
Wives died, were dropped like old shirts in some
    corner of country.
Said, "Mister," in bed, the child-bride; hadn't known
    what to find there;
Wept all the next morning for shame; took pleasure in
    silk; wore the keys to the pantry.

"Will die in these ditches if need be," wrote Bowie, at
    the Alamo.
And did, he whose left foot, soft-catting, came
    forward, and breath hissed:
Head back, gray eyes narrow, thumb flat along knife-
    blade, blade low.
"Great gentleman," said Henry Clay, "and a patriot."
    Portrait by Benjamin West.

Or take those, the nameless, of whom no portraits
    remain,
No locket or seal ring, though somewhere, broken
    and rusted,
In attic or earth, the long Decherd, stock rotten,
    has lain;
Or the mold-yellow Bible, God's Word, in which,
    in their strength, they had also trusted.

Some wrestled the angel, and took a fall by the corncrib.
Fought the brute, stomp-and-gouge, but knew they
     were doomed in that glory.
All night, in sweat, groaned; fell at last with spit red
     and a cracked rib.
How sweet then the tears! Thus gentled, they roved
     the dark land with their old story.

Some prospered, had black men and lands, and silver
     on table,
But remembered the owl call, the smell of burnt bear
     fat on dusk-air.
Loved family and friends, and stood it as long as able,
"But money and women, too much is ruination, am
     Arkansas-bound." So went there.

One of mine was a land shark, or so the book with
     scant praise
Denominates him, "a man large and shapeless,
Like a sack of potatoes set on a saddle," it says,
"Little learning but shrewd, not well trusted." Rides
     thus out of history, neck fat and napeless.

One saw Shiloh and such, got cranky, would fiddle all
     night.
The boys nagged for Texas. "God damn it, there's
     nothing, God damn it,

136

In Texas," but took wagons, went, and to prove he
    was right,
Stayed a year and a day, "hell, nothing in Texas," had
    proved it, came back to black vomit,

And died, and they died, and are dead, and now their
    voices
Come thin, like last cricket in frost-dark, in grass lost,
With nothing to tell us for our complexity of choices,
But beg us only one word to justify their own old
    life-cost.

So let us bend ear to them in this hour of lateness,
And what they are trying to say, try to understand,
And try to forgive them their defects, even their
    greatness,
For we are their children in the light of humanness,
    and under the shadow of God's closing hand.

MANIFESTO: THE MAD FARMER LIBERATION FRONT

Love the quick profit, the annual raise,
vacation with pay. Want more
of everything ready made. Be afraid
to know your neighbors and to die.
And you will have a window in your head.
Not even your future will be a mystery
any more. Your mind will be punched in a card
and shut away in a little drawer.
When they want you to buy something
they will call you. When they want you
to die for profit they will let you know.
So, friends, every day do something
that won't compute. Love the Lord.
Love the world. Work for nothing.
Take all that you have and be poor.
Love someone who does not deserve it.
Denounce the government and embrace
the flag. Hope to live in that free
republic for which it stands.
Give your approval to all you cannot
understand. Praise ignorance, for what man
has not encountered he has not destroyed.
Ask the questions that have no answers.
Invest in the millennium. Plant sequoias.

Say that your main crop is the forest
that you did not plant,
that you will not live to harvest.
Say that the leaves are harvested
when they have rotted into the mold.
Call that profit. Prophesy such returns.
Put your faith in the two inches of humus
that will build under the trees
every thousand years.
Listen to carrion — put your ear
close, and hear the faint chattering
of the songs that are to come.
Expect the end of the world. Laugh.
Laughter is immeasurable. Be joyful
though you have considered all the facts.
So long as women do not go cheap
for power, please women more than men.
Ask yourself: Will this satisfy
a woman satisfied to bear a child?
Will this disturb the sleep
of a woman near to giving birth?
Go with your love to the fields.
Lie easy in the shade. Rest your head
in her lap. Swear allegiance

to what is nighest your thoughts.
As soon as the generals and the politicos
can predict the motions of your mind,
lose it. Leave it as a sign
to mark the false trail, the way
you didn't go. Be like the fox
who makes more tracks than necessary,
some in the wrong direction.
Practice resurrection.

THE WARDEN SAID TO ME
THE OTHER DAY

The warden said to me the other day
(innocently, I think), "Say, etheridge,
why come the black boys don't run off
like the white boys do?"
I lowered my jaw and scratched my head
and said (innocently, I think), "Well, suh,
I ain't for sure, but I reckon it's cause
we ain't got no wheres to run to."

I HAVE WALKED A LONG TIME

i have walked a long time
much longer than death that splinters
wid her innuendos.
my life, ah my alien life,
is like an echo of nostalgia
bringen blue screens to bury clouds
rinsen wite stones stretched among the sea.

    you, man, will you remember me when i die?
    will you stare and stain my death and say
    i saw her dancen among swallows
    far from the world's obscenities?
    you, man, will you remember and cry?

and i have not loved.
always
while the body prowls
the soul catalogues each step;
while the unconscious unbridles feasts
the flesh knots toward the shore.
ah, i have not loved
wid legs stretched like stalks against sheets
wid stomachs drainen the piracy of oceans
wid mouths discarden the gelatin
to shake the sharp self.

i have walked by memory of others
between the blood night
and twilights
i have lived in tunnels
and fed the bloodless fish;
between the yellow rain
and ash,
i have heard the rattle
of my seed,
so time, like some pearl necklace embracen
a superior whore, converges
and the swift spider binds my breast.

you, man, will you remember me when i die?
will you stare and stain my death and say
i saw her applauden suns
far from the grandiose audience?
you, man, will you remember and cry?

SONIA SANCHEZ (1934–)   143

REMARKS ON COLOR

1. highway patched with blacktop, service station at the crossroads
2. cream soda in the popbox, man sitting on the popbox
3. a fully grown man
4. filthy toilets, just hold it a little while longer
5. shacks ringed with day lilies, then a columned house in shade
6. condensation off soybeans
7. someone known as Skeeter
8. his whole life
9. flatbed loaded with striped melons
10. Lopez's white car at JB's mother's house
11. katydids crepitating in the tall grass
12. gar wrapping itself in your line
13. gourds strung between poles
14. imagine a tribe of color-blind people, and there could easily be one, they would not have the same color concepts as we do
15. that's trumpet vine; that's what we call potato vine
16. no potatoes come of it though
17. no potatoes I know
18. I come back here about three years ago to see if I could eke out a living then I run on to Rhonda
19. help me Rhonda help help me Rhonda

20. E-Z on E-Z off
21. out of wedlock, wedlocked
22. planks nailed across kitchen doorway for a bar;
    living room turned into dance floor
23. drinking canned heat
24. the shit can make you permanently blind
25. sizzling nights
26. what do you suppose became of Fontella Bass
27. get your own sound then notes go with your
    sound – it's like a color, my color – I'm black
    brown with a little red-orange in my skin
28. red looks good on me
29. and yet we could imagine circumstances under
    which we would say, these people see other colors
    in addition to ours
30. what the Swede concluded: if you want to know
    what's the matter with blacks in America study the
    other side of the color line
31. I am just telling you what the man figured out
32. there is, after all, no commonly accepted criterion
    for what is a color unless it is one of our colors
33. check this:
34. at the time of his death Presley's was the second
    most reproduced image in the world
35. the first was Mickey Mouse

36. Lansky Brothers – down on Beale – outfitted the
    johns of Memphis
37. and Elvis
38. R-U ready for Jesus R-U packed up
39. just don't compare me to any white musicians
40. take me witcha man when you go

YELLOWHAMMER, MAGNOLIA, AND THE NATURAL STATE

POEMS OF ALABAMA, MISSISSIPPI AND ARKANSAS

BIRMINGHAM SUNDAY
(September 15, 1963)

Four little girls
Who went to Sunday School that day
And never came back home at all
But left instead
Their blood upon the wall
With spattered flesh
And bloodied Sunday dresses
Torn to shreds by dynamite
That China made aeons ago –
Did not know
That what China made
Before China was ever Red at all
Would ever redden with their blood
This Birmingham-on-Sunday wall.

Four tiny little girls
Who left their blood upon that wall,
In little graves today await
The dynamite that might ignite
The fuse of centuries of Dragon Kings
Whose tomorrow sings a hymn
The missionaries never taught Chinese
In Christian Sunday School
To implement the Golden Rule.

Four little girls
Might be awakened someday soon
By songs upon the breeze
As yet unfelt among magnolia trees.

THE IDEA OF ANCESTRY

1.

Taped to the wall of my cell are 47 pictures: 47 black
faces: my father, mother, grandmothers (1 dead), grand-
fathers (both dead), brothers, sisters, uncles, aunts,
cousins (1st and 2nd), nieces, and nephews. They stare
across the space at me sprawling on my bunk. I know
their dark eyes, they know mine. I know their style,
they know mine. I am all of them, they are all of me;
they are farmers, I am a thief, I am me, they are thee.

I have at one time or another been in love with my
     mother,
1 grandmother, 2 sisters, 2 aunts (1 went to the
     asylum),
and 5 cousins. I am now in love with a 7-yr-old niece
(she sends me letters in large block print, and
her picture is the only one that smiles at me).

I have the same name as 1 grandfather, 3 cousins,
     3 nephews,
and 1 uncle. The uncle disappeared when he was 15,
     just took
off and caught a freight (they say). He's discussed
     each year
when the family has a reunion, he causes uneasiness in

the clan, he is an empty space. My father's mother,
  who is 93
and who keeps the Family Bible with everybody's birth
  dates
(and death dates) in it, always mentions him. There is no
place in her Bible for "whereabouts unknown."

  2.
Each fall the graves of my grandfathers call me, the
  brown
hills and red gullies of mississippi send out their electric
messages, galvanizing my genes. Last yr/like a salmon
  quitting
the cold ocean – leaping and bucking up his birth
  stream/I
hitchhiked my way from LA with 16 caps in my pocket
  and a
monkey on my back. And I almost kicked it with the
  kinfolks.
I walked barefooted in my grandmother's backyard/I
  smelled the old
land and the woods/I sipped cornwhiskey from fruit
  jars with the men/
I flirted with the women/I had a ball till the caps ran out
and my habit came down. That night I looked at my
  grandmother

and split/my guts were screaming for junk/but I was almost
contented/I had almost caught up with me.
(The next day in Memphis I cracked a croaker's crib
     for a fix.)

This yr there is a gray stone wall damming my stream,
     and when
the falling leaves stir my genes, I pace my cell or flop
     on my bunk
and stare at 47 black faces across the space. I am all of
     them,
they are all of me, I am me, they are thee, and I have no
     children
to float in the space between.

JULIA TUTWILER STATE PRISON
FOR WOMEN

On the prison's tramped-hard Alabama clay
two green-clad women walk, hold hands,
and swing their arms as though they'll laugh,
meander at their common whim, and not
be forced to make a quarter turn each time
they reach a corner of the fence. Though they
can't really be as gentle as they seem
perhaps they're better lovers for their crimes,
the times they didn't think before acting –
or thought, and said to hell with the consequences.
Most are here for crimes of passion.
They've killed for jealousy, anger, love,
and now they sleep a lot. Who else
is dangerous for love – for love
or hate or anything? Who else would risk
a ten-year walk inside the fenced in edge
of a field stripped clean of soybeans or wheat?
Skimming in from the west and pounding hard
across the scoured land, a summer rain
raises puffs of dust with its first huge drops.
It envelopes the lingering women. They hesitate,
then race, hand in hand, for shelter, laughing.

SWEEP

The two Garnett brothers who run the Shell station
　　here,
who are working separately just now,
one hunched under the rear axle of Skippy Smith's
　　Peterbilt tractor,
the other humming as he loosens the clamps
to replace my ruptured heater hoses,
have aged twenty years since I saw them last
and want only to talk of high school
and who has died from each class.
Seamless gray sky, horns from the four-lane,
the lot's oil slicks rainbowing and dimpling with rain.
I have been home for three days, listening to an obituary.
The names of relatives met once,
of men from the plant where he works,
click like distant locks on my father's lips.
I know that it is death that obsesses him
more than football or weather
and that cancer is far too prevalent
in this green valley of herbicides and chemical factories.
Now Mike, the younger brother,
lifts from my engine compartment
a cluster of ruined hoses,
twisted and curled together like a nest of blacksnakes,
and whistles as he forages in the rack

for more. Slowly, the way things work down here,
while I wait and the rain plinks on the rims of
    overturned tires,
he and my father trade the names of the dead:
Bill Farrell for Albert Dotson,
Myles Hammond, the quick tackle of our football team,
for Don Appleton, the slow, redheaded one.
By the time the rack is exhausted
I'm thinking if I lived here all year I'd buy American,
I'd drive a truck, and I'm thinking
of football and my father's and Mike's words
staking out an absence I know I won't reclaim.
Because I don't get home much anymore,
I notice the smallest scintilla of change,
every burnt-out trailer and newly paved road,
and the larger, slower change
that is exponential,
that strangeness, like the unanticipated face
of my aunt, shrunken and perversely stylish
under the turban she wore after chemotherapy.
But mostly it's the wait, one wait after another,
and I'm dropping back deep in the secondary
under the chill and pipe smoke of a canceled October
while the sweep rolls toward me from the line of
    scrimmage,
and Myles Hammond, who will think too slowly
and turn his air-force jet into the Arizona desert,

156

and Don Appleton, who will drive out on a country road
for a shotgun in his mouth, are cut down,
and I'm shifting on the balls of my feet,
bobbing and saving one nearly hopeless feint,
one last plunge for the blockers
and the ballcarrier who follows the sweep,
and it comes, and comes on.

THE OZARK ODES

Lake Return

Maybe you have to be from there to hear it sing:
Give me your waterweeds, your nipples,
your shoehorn and your four-year letter jacket,
the molded leftovers from the singed pot.
Now let me see your underside, white as fishes.
I lower my gaze against your clitoral light.

Rent House

O the hours I lay on the bed
looking at the knotted pine
in the added-on room
where he kept his old Corona,
the poet with the big lips –
where we slept together.

Somebody's Mother

Flour rose from her shoulders
as she walked out of her kitchen.
The report of the screendoor,
the scrapdog unperturbed.
Afternoon sky pinking up.

Table Grace

Bless Lou Vindie, bless Truman,
bless the fields
of rocks, the brown recluse
behind the wallpaper,
chink in the plaster,
bless cowchips, bless brambles
and the copperhead, the honey locusts
shedding their frilly flower
on waxed cars, bless them
the loudmouths and goiters
and dogs with the mange,
bless each and every one
for doing their utmost.
Yea, for they have done
their naturally suspicious part.

Girlhood

Mother had one. She and Bernice racing for the river
to play with their paperdolls
because they did not want any big ears
to hear what their paperdolls were fixing to say.

Judge

Had a boyhood. Had his own rooster. Name of Andy.
Andy liked to ride in Judge's overall bib.
Made him bald. This really vexed Judge's old daddy.

Arkansas Towns

Acorn
Back Gate
Bald Knob
Ben Hur
Biggers
Blue Ball
Congo
Delight
Ebony
Eros
Fifty-Six
Figure Five
Flippin
Four Sisters
Goshen
Greasy Corner
Havana
Hector
Hogeye

160

Ink
Jenny Lind
Little Flock
Marked Tree
Mist
Monkey Run
Moscow
Nail
Okay
Ozone
Rag Town
Ratio
Seaton Dump
Self
Snowball
Snow Lake
Sweet Home
Three Brothers
Three Folks
Twist
Urbanette
Whisp
Yellville
Zent

Lake Return

Where the sharp rock on shore
give way to the hairy rock in the shallows,
we enlisted in the rise and fall of love.
His seed broadcast like short, sweet grass.
Nothing came up there.

Dry County Bar

Bourbon not fit to put on a sore. No women enter;
their men collect in every kind of weather
with no shirts on whatsoever.

Cafe at the Junction

The way she sees him
how the rain doesn't let up

4-ever blue and vigilant
as a clock in a corner

peeling the label from his bottle
hungry but not touching food

as she turns down the wet lane
where oaks vault the road

The Boyfriend

wakes in darkness of morning
and visits the water

lowering his glad body
onto a flat rock

the spiders rearrange
themselves underneath

Remedy

Sty sty leave my eye,
go to the next feller passing by.

Porch

I can still see Cuddihy's sisters
trimming the red tufts
under one another's arms.

Bait Shop

Total sales today: 3 doz. minnows, 1/2 doz. crawdaddies,
    4 lead lures,
loaf of light bread, pack of Raleighs, 3 bags of barbecued
    pork skins.

Fred

One of your more irascible poets from the hill country.
Retired to his mother's staunch house
in Little Rock after her death; began to build
a desk for Arthur. Beautiful piece
of work. For a friend. Beautiful.
Drinking less, putting on a few pounds.

Lake Return

Why I come here: need for a bottom, something to
    refer to;
where all things visible and invisible commence to
    swarm.

for Fred

THE FARTHEST NORTH
SOUTHERN TOWN

My hairdresser Frank's own hair's cut punk
today, livid as a ruffled bird.
He tells me about his brother-in-law
on the police force who tells him how
the cops punch out the punks on Main Street,
and get away with it, too. They got
these leather gloves, he says, with brass
inside, so no bruises show, and even
if there are some, they're gone
by the time the trial comes up, or the judge
will say you might have fallen down
stairs. This town is the farthest-north
Southern town, Frank says, switching scissors,
and nobody wants to argue with the mayor,
who appoints the police chief, and so on,
like a ricochet bullet, down
to your basic level of cop who takes
his shift to count the number of times
the same car cruises Main Street
in an hour. Three time's the limit.
Then out he comes, his cruiser flashing
red and blue. They mostly nail
the ones with racing stripes and mag
wheels, not the little Subaru wagons,

Frank says, spraying mousse in his palm,
lifting my hair to an elegant panic.
We are squared off in the mirror.
What's more, the law says they can still
hang you, here, he goes on, for stealing
a horse. I won't, I say. I won't.

THE GOSPEL BIRD

I. *Superman*

Dressed in a superman suit
On the front porch of Chitum's store
I told all the Negroes "I can fly"
And jumped off the high end.

A German crop duster crashed.
A chicken ran out of the hole
And shit on a rusty three-penny nail,
Then ducked back under the stoop.

Blood and chickenshit
Dripping out of the hole
Into the good hand,
Jimmy says, "What you saving it for?"

He went to the fire
And nobody was studying me
But toad frogs and a dog.
"Whoa somebody! I done cut my hand off."

Nobody came but the Rollie Pollie man,
Skipping chuck-holes and swinging coal oil
In a copper-wired Co-cola bottle.
He says, "I'll tend to you boy, I'll tend to you."

II. *Fire*

Chitum's cripple nigger carpenter
Ate porch bugs and did magic.
He had a police dog that brought him
Dead chickens in the night.

"Put hog lard on an oak tree,
Steal me whiskey and coal oil,
And this dog will bring your chicken back."
I wanted that bird.

"Lock Jaw and penicillin all the same,
Kill the chicken to kill the pain."
I got the nigger a fifth of gin
And he sent his dog after the bird.

The Rollie Pollie man told me how it was:
"The blood spurt out when that son-of-a-bitch
Chitum blew my crooked-necked
Chicken-killing dog in half.

"Black gnats was dying in the blood,
Some already drowned, I took coat wire
And drug him deep into the Diamond Woods."
My hand and Chitum's store burned that night.

III. *Fly Away, Fly Away*

My father talked like he was singing
When he bought the burnt-out land and store,
But all I cared about was
The one thousand chickens in the deal.

He said to kill all the birds
And sell the meat to the levee camps
Up and down the river.
The Rollie Pollie man was on the run.

Jimmy was wringing their necks
And making a clean kill,
But I was knocking
Their heads off with a tomato stick

Every time I connected
I'd go check the bird out.
They'd bat their wings and squirt blood,
Winking at me.

I was busting green heads off ducks, too.
Jimmy had to hold me back.
"What's wrong with you, Superman?"
"Fly away, fly away, Gospel Bird," I cried.

FOUR HUNDRED MOURNERS

The sizes of the crowds in those burn-baby-burn days
were at best estimates, depending on who –
the police, the press, the thousands in protest –
was counting. The body count, we called it,
and after the arrest we were lined up
alphabetically for fingerprints and phone calls.
It wasn't all that much, though the numbers
made a difference since they argued significance.
That was later, at the dead end of the sixties,
the rallies against the war mixed with the killings
of the Kennedys and King and the nuclear meltdown
of democracy at the convention in Chicago.
But at the beginning of the decade
it was man-on-the-moon, hand-on-the-heart.
Ralph Abernathy, who had recruited most of us,
came by one day just to say hello.
We were on the white side of the table,
the soon-to-be-eligible black voters on the other.
Greenville was as liberal as it got in Mississippi,
the Delta almost as ancient as the flooding of the Nile.
The names, the spellings, the signatures,
like maps of a world once flat.
And the heat and the dog's-breath weight of the air
and the wet dust needlework of pine.
People had died here under a different register,

as thousands more thousands of nautical miles
southeast would die who had not voted.
Ralph said the numbers finally didn't matter,
the idea of change was enough.
He meant "an idea whose time has come."
The few new voters each seemed wise and old,
older than anyone we knew, older than parents
or grandparents, older than the country
or anger's life expectancy.
The had looked into the sun,
they had looked into it a long time.
The Carter family newspaper spoke of joy
with sometimes grief, as if the happiness
of change felt like a passage.
This is fifty years now, gone.
It's crazy that so much of it came back to me
witnessing the funeral of a child.
The countless car cortege wound through the town's
winter wastes as if the hearse could not quite find its way.
There is no end to the death of a child,
so that when we detoured past her elementary school
everyone was out in the cold, in the hundreds, waving.

STANLEY PLUMLY (1939–)   171

PROVIDENCE

What's left is footage: the hours before
        Camille, 1969 – hurricane
                parties, palm trees leaning
in the wind,
        fronds blown back,

a woman's hair. Then after:
        the vacant lots,
        boats washed ashore, a swamp

where graves had been. I recall

how we huddled all night in our small house,
        moving between rooms,
                emptying pots filled with rain.

Then next day, our house –
        on its cinderblocks – seemed to float

        in the flooded yard: no foundation

beneath us, nothing I could see
        tying us   to the land.
        In the water, our reflection
                        trembled,
disappeared
when I bent to touch it.

TRIP HOP

I'll pack my toothbrush
and my cyanide molar
the iPhone the car-seats
and a tactical stroller

I'll pack a snack-bag
with the Kraft food groups
and white flags for me
and black for my troops

I'll pack a fresh pack
of Shark double-edge blades
my boy's Razr scooter
and my girl's blue shades

I'll pack doses of patience
and some Kevlar smiles
check our air and our fluids
our gauges and dials

and we'll hit I-40
in our old green Accord
there'll be collateral damage
and we might get bored

but we won't need TomTom
to know where we're headed
a theme park they dream of
a theme park I've dreaded

and if we ever get home
and if our home still stands
I'll unpack my dark heart
and Purell my hands

PORTRAIT OF UNKNOWN PROVENANCE
OF DIDO ELIZABETH BELLE LINDSAY,
THE CHILD OF AN UNKNOWN AFRICAN
WOMAN AND ADMIRAL SIR JOHN
LINDSAY, AND HER COUSIN, THE
LADY ELIZABETH MURRAY,*
c. 1779

A Black came in after dinner and sat with the ladies ...
Lord M ... calls her Dido, which I suppose is all the
name she has. He knows he has been reproached for
showing fondness for her ...

> From *The Diary and Letters of*
> *His Excellency Thomas Hutchinson,*
> August 1779

Dido moves quickly –
as from the Latin *anime.*

Breath or soul.
Beside her, the generations-free kin,

* Both girls in the portrait are the great-nieces of William
Murray, First Earl of Mansfield and Lord Chief Justice of the
King's Bench. Mansfield issued the historic *Somerset* ruling of
1772, which made it unlawful for slaves to be forcibly taken from
Britain and resold into slavery.

a biscuit figurine in pink.
Dido standing in irony –

the lowest are taller here –
Elizabeth should provide

an unkind contrast: pretty, blond,
pale in uncovered places –

but no.
The painter worships the quickened other.

Dido, his coquette of deep-dish
dimples, his careless, bright love.

Forget history.
She's a teenager.

We know what that means.
Cocky, stupid about reality.

No thought of babies –
feathers in her arms.

She might wave them, clearing
dead mothers from the air –

and surely, she's special –
her uncle dressed her with care,

hid her from triangles and seas
outside this walled garden.

Let her be.
Please.

No Dying Mythical Queen
weaving a vivid, troubled skin –

but Dido, full of girlhood,
and Elizabeth reaching

a hand. *Behave, cousin,*
she begs.

Don't run away from me.

BEAUS AND BELLES

We were such light sleepers
Such long distance believers
— NIKKI FINNEY

SONG FOR A DARK GIRL

Way Down South in Dixie
   (Break the heart of me)
They hung my black young lover
   To a cross roads tree.

Way Down South in Dixie
   (Bruised body high in air)
I asked the white Lord Jesus
   What was the use of prayer.

Way Down South in Dixie
   (Break the heart of me)
Love is a naked shadow
   On a gnarled and naked tree.

LANGSTON HUGHES (1902–1967)

PIAZZA PIECE

– I am a gentleman in a dustcoat trying
To make you hear. Your ears are soft and small
And listen to an old man not at all,
They want the young men's whispering and sighing.
But see the roses on your trellis dying
And hear the spectral singing of the moon;
For I must have my lovely lady soon,
I am a gentleman in a dustcoat trying.

– I am a lady young in beauty waiting
Until my truelove comes, and then we kiss.
But what grey man among the vines is this
Whose words are dry and faint as in a dream?
Back from my trellis, Sir, before I scream!
I am a lady young in beauty waiting.

PAUSE, IN FLIGHT

Late August. The wind stays awake all night
Thinking of autumn. The crickets wonder
Out loud about the future . . . Damn the past.
Damn the past . . . Fall is yonder,
The constellation we are travelling to.
No, we are where it is travelling to
From a distance, a time, long overdue,
Extinguished before the hunter put
The gun over his shoulder. Will these trees
Be the last to receive
This light? The crickets, apprehensive,
Give ear. This light, this autumn, this hunter –
Comes already dead. Who
Flutters featherless into the leaves?

BURNED MAN

When I was twelve, a man was burned
not quite to death at my father's
factory. Recovered enough
to walk the town, he didn't know
what to do with himself – a ghost
whose scarred, fire bubbled face made you
look away, though not my father
who felt responsible and so wouldn't
refuse the man's eyes when they fell
upon him. The burned man held no
grudge, thought the accident his
own fault, and sought my father out
as the one whose eyes told him yes,
he was still alive.

So they held long
conversations on the post office
stoop, which I observed from the car
where I waited, where I could read
my father's stiff shoulders, the way
he clutched the mail, how he tilted
his head, even his smile that was
in truth a grimace. I knew just
what my mother knew – my father
had to let himself be tortured
once or twice a week, whenever

Bernard Sawyers saw him in town,
lifted his claw of a hand, rasped
out his greeting that sounded like
a raven that'd been taught to say
Hello, Mr. Huddle, how are you?
They'd stand there talking in the town's
blazing sunlight, the one whom fire
had taken to the edge of death
and the other invisibly
burning while they passed the time of day.

EVERYTHING GOOD BETWEEN
MEN AND WOMEN

has been written in mud and butter
and barbecue sauce. The walls and
the floors used to be gorgeous.
The socks off-white and a near match.
The quince with fire blight
but we get two pints of jelly
in the end. Long walks strengthen
the back. You with a fever blister
and myself with a sty. Eyes
have we and we are forever prey
to each other's teeth. The torrents
go over us. Thunder has not harmed
anyone we know. The river coursing
through us is dirty and deep. The left
hand protects the rhythm. Watch
your head. No fires should be
unattended. Especially when wind. Each
receives a free swiss army knife.
The first few tongues are clearly
preparatory. The impression
made by yours I carry to my grave. It is
just so sad so creepy so beautiful.
Bless it. We have so little time
to learn, so much ... The river
courses dirty and deep. Cover the lettuce.
Call it a night. O soul. Flow on. Instead.

186   C. D. WRIGHT (1949–)

MOUNTAINS
AND THE
OLD DOMINION

POEMS OF WEST VIRGINIA AND VIRGINIA

THE SOUL AND BODY OF JOHN BROWN

Multitudes, multitudes in the valley of decision!
— JOEL IV : 14

His life is in the body of the living.
When they hanged him the first time, his image leaped
into the blackened air. His grave was the floating faces
of the crowd, and he refused them in release,
rose open-eyed to autumn, a fanatic
beacon of fierceness leaping to meet them there,
match the white prophets of the storm,
the streaming meteors of the war.

Dreaming Ezekiel, threaten me alive!

Scissors! Why don't you rip up that guitar?
Or must we listen to those blistering strings?

The trial of heroes follows their execution. The striding
wind of western nations carried new rain, new lightning,
destroyed in magnificence with noon shining straight
    down
swaying the fiery pines. He wanted freedom. Could not
    himself be free
until more grace reached a corroded world. Our guilt
    his own.
Under the cloak of the century drops the trap —

There! tall in October's fruition-fire stand
three images of himself, one as he stood on the ground,
one as he stood on sudden air, the third
receding to our fatal topmost hills
faded through dying altitudes, and low
through faces living under the dregs of the air,
deprived childhood and thwarted youth and change:
    fantastic sweetness gone to rags
    and incorruptible anger blurred by age.

Compel the steps of lovers, watch them lie silvery
attractive in naked embrace over the brilliant gorge,
and open them to love: enlarge their welcome
to sharp-faced countrysides, vicious familiar windows
where lopped-off worlds say *I am promise*, holding
the stopgap slogans of a thin season offering only
the false initials, blind address, dummy name –
enemies who reply in smiles, mild slavers, moderate
    whores.
– There is a gorge to remember, where the soldiers
    came
in a terrible answer of lechery after death.
– He said at last, with a living perfect look,
"I designed to have done the same thing again
on a larger scale." Sleepless, he sees his tree
grow in the land, a wish to leap these mountains.
They are not mountains, but men and women sleeping.

O my scene! my mother!
America who offers many births.

Over the tiers of barriers, compel the steps of armies
who will arrive with horizon sharpness rising
in quick embrace toward the people who greet them,
        love
faltering in our hills among the symptoms of ice,
small lights of the shifting winter, the rapid snow-blue
        stars.
This must be done by armies. Nothing is free.
        He knows
direct attacks, refuses to speak again,
            "If I tell them the truth,
                they will say I speak in symbols."

White rhetoric of landscapes gives him his nakedness
reflected in counties of naked who shiver and stare at
        fires,
their backs to the face that unrolls new worlds around
        them.
They go down the valleys. They shamble in the streets.
Blind to the sun-storming image echoed in their eyes.
They dread the surface of their victim life,
lying helpless and savage in shade parks,
            asking the towers only what beggars dare:
            food, fire, water, and air.

Spring: the great hieroglyph: the mighty, whose first hour
collects the winter invalids, whose cloudless
pastures train swarms of mutable apple-trees
to blond delusions of light, the touch of whiter
more memorable breasts each evening, the resistant
male shoulders riding under sold terrible eyes.
The soldier-face persists, the victorious head
kissing those breasts asks for more miracles –
Untarnished hair! Set them free! "Without the snap of
    a gun –"
More failures – but the season is a garden after sickness;
       Then the song begins,
       "The clearing of the sky
       brings fulness to heroes –
       Call Death out of the city
       and ring the summer in."

Whether they sleep alone. Whether they understand
    darkness
of mine or tunnel or store. Whether they lay branches
with Western skill to entice their visions out of fire.
Whether she lie awake, whether he walk in guilt
down silenced corridors, leaving no fingerprints.
Whether he weaken searching for power in pamphlets,
or shut out every fantasy but the fragile eyelid to
       commemorate delight . . .
       They believe in their dreams.

They more and more, secretly, tell their dreams.
They listen oftener for certain words, look deeper
in faces for features of one remembered image.
They almost forget the face. They cannot miss the look.
It waits until faces have gathered darkness,
and country guitars a wide and subtle music.
It rouses love. It has mastered its origin:
        Death was its method. It will surpass its
        furious birth when it is known again.

      Dreaming Ezekiel, threaten me alive!

Greengrown with the sun on it. All the living summer.
They tell their dreams on the cool hill reclining,
after the daytime gestures repeat the toothless cannon,
the spite of tractors over a salvable field.
The cities of horror are down. These are called born,
and Hungry Hill's to them a plain again.
They stand in the factory, deal out identical
gestures of reaching – cathedral-color-rose
resumes the bricks as the walls go leaning – bend
away from the windows, blank in bellwavering air,
reach out, mechanical cat's-claw reaping sky.

      I know your face, deepdrowned
      prophet, and seablown eyes.

Darkflowing peoples. A tall tree, prophet, fallen,
your arms in their flesh laid on the mountains, all
your branches in the scattered valleys down.
Your boughs lie broken in channels of the land,
dim anniversaries written on many clouds.
– There is no partial help. Lost in the face of a child,
lost in the factory repetitions, lost
on the steel plateaus, in a ghost distorted.
– Calling More Life. In all the harm calling.
Pointing disaster of death and lifting up the bone,
heroic drug and the intoxication gone.

> I see your mouth calling
> before the words arrive.

The strings repeat it, buzz of guitars, a streamy
summernoon song, the whitelight of the meaning
filling American valleys. More life, saying: this rich,
this hatred, this Hallelloo – risk it upon yourselves.
– Free all the dangers of promise, clear the image
of freedom for the body of the world. –
After the tree is fallen and has become the land,
when the hand in the earth declined rises and touches air,
after the walls go down and all the faces turn,
the diamond shoals of eyes demanding life
deep in the prophet eyes, a wish to be again
threatened alive, in agonies of decision
part of the nation of a fanatic sun.

A SHORT HISTORY OF THE SHADOW

Thanksgiving, dark of the moon.
Nothing down here in the underworld but vague
    shapes and black holes,
Heaven resplendent but virtual
Above me,
        trees stripped and triple-wired like Irish harps.
Lights on Pantops and Free Bridge mirror the
    eastern sky.
Under the bridge is the river,
           the red Rivanna.
Under the river's redemption, it says in the book,
It says in the book,
Through water and fire the whole place becomes purified,
The visible by the visible, the hidden by what is hidden.

*   *   *

Each word, as someone once wrote, contains the
    universe.
The visible carries all the invisible on its back.
Tonight, in the unconditional, what moves in the
    long-limbed grasses,
        what touches me
As though I didn't exist?
What is it that keeps on moving,
        a tiny pillar of smoke

195

Erect on its hind legs,
                    loose in the hollow grasses?
A word I don't know yet, a little word, containing
        infinity,
Noiseless and unrepentant, in sift through the dry grass.
Under the tongue is the utterance.
Under the utterance is the fire, and then the only end
        of fire.
                        *   *   *

Only Dante, in Purgatory, casts a shadow,
L'ombra della carne, the shadow of flesh –
                            everyone else *is* one.
The darkness that flows from the world's body,
        gloomy spot,
Pre-dogs our footsteps, and follows us,
                            diaphanous bodies
Watching the nouns circle, and watching the verbs
        circle,
Till one of them enters the left ear and becomes a
        shadow
Itself, sweet word in the unwaxed ear.
This is a short history of the shadow, one part of us
        that's real.
This is the way the world looks
In late November,
        no leaves on the trees, no ledge to foil the lightfall.

                        *   *   *

No ledge in early December either, and no ice,
La Niña unhosing the heat pump
                              up from the Gulf,
Orange Crush sunset over the Blue Ridge,
No shadow from anything as evening gathers its
    objects
And eases into earshot.
Under the influx the outtake,
                        Leon Battista Alberti says,
Some lights are from stars, some from the sun
And moon, and other lights are from fires.
The light from the stars makes the shadow equal to
    the body.
Light from fire makes it greater,
      there, under the tongue, there, under the utterance.

VIRGINIA BACKYARD; JULY

Waking late, still inside a humid
heat-drenched dream that's not unlike
Keats' "sweet unrest," I walk
out past the fence where purple morning
glories have closed up into tight
buttons of color. Wild strawberry
plants I picked this spring are mostly
covered now by a thick new growth
of honeysuckle; kept from sun
the patch won't last. An indigo
bunting pauses on a dogwood twig.
Folding back golden petals, a sunflower
permits a first honeybee to wade
the wide, uneven expanse of a seedface
that spirals to a lime-green, pubic tuft.

IN THE LOOP

I heard from people after the shootings. People
I knew well or barely or not at all. Largely
the same message: how horrible it was, how little
there was to say about how horrible it was.
People wrote, called, mostly e-mailed
because they know I teach at Virginia Tech,
to say, there's nothing to say. Eventually
I answered these messages: there's nothing
to say back except of course there's nothing
to say, thank you for your willingness
to say it. Because this was about nothing.
A boy who felt that he was nothing,
who erased and entered that erasure, and guns
that are good for nothing, and talk of guns
that is good for nothing, and spring
that is good for flowers, and Jesus for some,
and scotch for others, and "and" for me
in this poem, "and" that is good
for sewing the minutes together, which otherwise
go about going away, bereft of us and us
of them. Like a scarf left on a train and nothing
like a scarf left on a train. As if the train,
empty of everything but a scarf, still opens
its doors at every stop, because this

is what a train does, this is what a man does
with his hand on a lever, because otherwise,
why the lever, why the hand, and then it was over,
and then it had just begun.

SONNET FOR HER LABOR

My Aunt Nita's kitchen was immaculate and dark,
and she was always bending to the sink
below the window where the shadows off the bulk
of Laurel Mountain rose up to the brink
of all the sky she saw from there. She clattered
pots on countertops wiped clean of coal dust,
fixed three meals a day, fried meat, mixed batter
for buckwheat cakes, hauled water, in what seemed lust
for labor. One March evening, after cleaning,
she lay down to rest and died. I can see Uncle Ed,
his fingers twined at his plate for the blessing;
my Uncle Craig leaning back, silent in red
galluses. No one said a word to her. All that food
and cleanliness. No one ever told her it was good.

ROANOKE PASTORALE

Cardinal, goldfinch, titmouse, turkey buzzard –
dear companions of my afternoons –
above this field, high clouds dream of blizzards

to snow me in till spring ends my solitude.
Sober's my binge now, nature my saloon.
Wren, mourning dove, house finch, turkey buzzard –

for your entertainment, I sing the words
of old fifties songs, use baby talk, croon
as I walk the field beneath great blizzard-

dreaming clouds. You gaudy pretties, sweet birds
of my senior years – my later's my soon.
Catbirds flit through cedars in the graveyard,

turkey buzzards swirl their patterns overhead,
across the mountainside sunlight bows a tune
rising to blue eternity but heard

by the heron fishing the creek, wizard
of stillness, creature designed by the moon.
Bluebird, jay, chipping sparrow, turkey buzzard,
clouds, and field – I dream this life, walk this world.

MORE NOTES ON THE THEORY OF
AMERICAN DEGENERACY

It's going to take a lot more than a moose
this time to convince the French that this country
isn't withered & rife with noxious vapors.
The Republic's going to hell in a hand basket.
All the poets say so. Though on second thought,
a moose might not be a bad start. What with that
      high-speed train
and all, let's take him live this time. Forget about the
      French.
Let's walk him right through front doors of the House
of Representatives. Knock. Like we're showing up
for the State of the Union. Antlers swinging, hooves
      skidding
marble. Seven feet tall. Behold! Of course then there'll
      be a debate
between Alaska and Wyoming on the origins of this
      moose.
And the South Dakotans will raise the question of bison.
Point of order, the New Jersey delegation will propose
an amendment to substitute a horse. Or an armadillo.
A golden bear. A badger or a ruffled grouse.
The Arizona delegation will move to see his papers.
Then some tired soul from the back bench:
      I yield my time

to the gentleman from Virginia & the lady from
 Oregon.
You: Behold the moose. Me: A deep curtsy, knee to
 the floor.
Yes, behold. Nunc dimittis, Domine.

SUNSHINE AND PEACHES

POEMS OF FLORIDA AND GEORGIA

ORANGE BUDS BY MAIL FROM FLORIDA

A lesser proof than old Voltaire's, yet greater,
Proof of this present time, and thee, thy broad
    expanse, America,
To my plain Northern hut, in outside clouds and snow,
Brought safely for a thousand miles o'er land and tide,
Some three days since on their own soil live sprouting,
Now here their sweetness through my room unfolding,
A bunch of orange buds by mail from Florida.

WALT WHITMAN (1819–1892)

THE IDEA OF ORDER AT KEY WEST

She sang beyond the genius of the sea.
The water never formed to mind or voice,
Like a body wholly body, fluttering
Its empty sleeves; and yet its mimic motion
Made constant cry, caused constantly a cry,
That was not ours although we understood,
Inhuman, of the veritable ocean.

The sea was not a mask. No more was she.
The song and water were not medleyed sound
Even if what she sang was what she heard,
Since what she sang was uttered word by word.
It may be that in all her phrases stirred
The grinding water and the gasping wind;
But it was she and not the sea we heard.

For she was the maker of the song she sang.
The ever-hooded, tragic-gestured sea
Was merely a place by which she walked to sing.
Whose spirit is this? we said, because we knew
It was the spirit that we sought and knew
That we should ask this often as she sang.

If it was only the dark voice of the sea
That rose, or even colored by many waves;

If it was only the outer voice of sky
And cloud, of the sunken coral water-walled,
However clear, it would have been deep air,
The heaving speech of air, a summer sound
Repeated in a summer without end
And sound alone. But it was more than that,
More even than her voice, and ours, among
The meaningless plungings of water and the wind,
Theatrical distances, bronze shadows heaped
On high horizons, mountainous atmospheres
Of sky and sea.

           It was her voice that made
The sky acutest at its vanishing.
She measured to the hour its solitude.
She was the single artificer of the world
In which she sang. And when she sang, the sea,
Whatever self it had, became the self
That was her song, for she was the maker. Then we,
As we beheld her striding there alone,
Knew that there never was a world for her
Except the one she sang and, singing, made.

Ramon Fernandez, tell me, if you know,
Why, when the singing ended and we turned
Toward the town, tell why the glassy lights,

The lights in the fishing boats at anchor there,
As the night descended, tilting in the air,
Mastered the night and portioned out the sea,
Fixing emblazoned zones and fiery poles,
Arranging, deepening, enchanting night.

Oh! Blessed rage for order, pale Ramon,
The maker's rage to order words of the sea,
Words of the fragrant portals, dimly-starred,
And of ourselves and of our origins,
In ghostlier demarcations, keener sounds.

GEORGIA DUSK

The sky, lazily disdaining to pursue
    The setting sun, too indolent to hold
    A lengthened tournament for flashing gold,
Passively darkens for night's barbecue,

A feast of moon and men and barking hounds,
    An orgy for some genius of the South
    With blood-hot eyes and cane-lipped scented mouth,
Surprised in making folk-songs from soul sounds.

The sawmill blows its whistle, buzz-saws stop,
    And silence breaks the bud of knoll and hill,
    Soft settling pollen where plowed lands fulfill
Their early promise of a bumper crop.

Smoke from the pyramidal sawdust pile
    Curls up, blue ghosts of trees, tarrying low
    Where only chips and stumps are left to show
The solid proof of former domicile.

Meanwhile, the men, with vestiges of pomp,
    Race memories of king and caravan,
    High-priests, an ostrich, and a juju-man,
Go singing through the footpaths of the swamp.

Their voices rise . . . the pine trees are guitars,
     Strumming, pine-needles fall like sheets of rain . . .
     Their voices rise . . . the chorus of the cane
Is caroling a vesper to the stars . . .

O singers, resinous and soft your songs
     Above the sacred whisper of the pines,
     Give virgin lips to cornfield concubines,
Bring dreams of Christ to dusky cane-lipped throngs.

DISCOVERY
for Katherine Jackson

The week the latest rocket went
up, a pod (if that's the word)
of manatees, come upriver
to Blue Spring where it's
always warm, could be seen
lolling, jacketed, elephantine,
on the weedy borderline
between drowsing and waking,
breathing and drowning.
As they came up for air,

one by one, they seemed numb,
torpid, quite incurious. No
imagining these sirenians
dangerously singing. Or
gazing up yearningly. (So much
for the Little Mermaid.) True,
the long-lashed little ones
might have been trademarked
Cute by the likes of Walt Disney.
His world's over that way,

suitably for a peninsula where
the cozy mythologies we've
swindled ourselves with, on
taking things easy, might even
come true: sun-kissed nakedness
on the beach, year-round, guilt-free
hibiscus and oranges, fountains
welling up through the limestone,
the rumor of Ponce de León, having
found the one he was looking for,

living at ease in, some say
Boca Raton, others Cádiz. A last
bedtime placebo? Still, we keep
looking up. That clear morning,
just warm enough for a liftoff,
the fabulous itself could be seen
unwieldily, jacket by jacket,
in the act of shedding, as
a snake does its husk, or
a celebrant his vestments:

the fiery, the arrowy tip of it,
of the actual going invisible,
trailing its vaporous, ribboning
frond as from a kelp bed,
the umbilical roar of it

stumbling behind, while up in
the belly of it, out of their
element, jacketed, lolling
and treading, the discoverers
soar, clumsy in space suits.

What are we anyhow, we warmth-
hungry, breast-seeking animals?
At Blue Spring, a day or so later,
one of the manatees, edging
toward discovery, nudged a canoe,
and from across the wet, warm,
dimly imaginable tightrope,
let itself be touched.

FLORIDA

The state with the prettiest name,
the state that floats in brackish water,
held together by mangrove roots
that bear while living oysters in clusters,
and when dead strew white swamps with skeletons,
dotted as if bombarded, with green hummocks
like ancient cannon-balls sprouting grass.
The state full of long S-shaped birds, blue and white,
and unseen hysterical birds who rush up the scale
every time in a tantrum.
Tanagers embarrassed by their flashiness,
and pelicans whose delight it is to clown;
who coast for fun on the strong tidal currents
in and out among the mangrove islands
and stand on the sand-bars drying their damp gold
     wings
on sun-lit evenings.
Enormous turtles, helpless and mild,
die and leave their barnacled shells on the beaches,
and their large white skulls with round eye-sockets
twice the size of a man's.
The palm trees clatter in the stiff breeze
like the bills of the pelicans. The tropical rain comes
     down
to freshen the tide-looped strings of fading shells:

Job's Tear, the Chinese Alphabet, the scarce Junonia,
parti-colored pectins and Ladies' Ears,
arranged as on a gray rag of rotted calico,
the buried Indian Princess's skirt;
with these the monotonous, endless, sagging coast-line
is delicately ornamented.

Thirty or more buzzards are drifting down, down, down,
over something they have spotted in the swamp,
in circles like stirred-up flakes of sediment
sinking through water.
Smoke from woods-fires filters fine blue solvents.
On stumps and dead trees the charring is like black
     velvet.
The mosquitoes
go hunting to the tune of their ferocious obbligatos.
After dark, the fireflies map the heavens in the marsh
until the moon rises.
Cold white, not bright, the moonlight is coarse-meshed,
and the careless, corrupt state is all black specks
too far apart, and ugly whites; the poorest
post-card of itself.
After dark, the pools seem to have slipped away.
The alligator, who has five distinct calls:
friendliness, love, mating, war, and a warning –
whimpers and speaks in the throat
of the Indian Princess.

ELIZABETH BISHOP (1911–1979)   217

UNDER THE VULTURE TREE

We have all seen them circling pastures,
have looked up from the mouth of a barn, a pine
      clearing,
the fences of our own backyards, and have stood
amazed by the one slow wing beat, the endless
      dihedral drift.
But I had never seen so many so close, hundreds,
every limb of the dead oak feathered black,

and I cut the engine, let the river grab the jon boat
and pull it toward the tree.
The black leaves shined, the pink fruit blossomed
red, ugly as a human heart.
Then, as I passed under their dream, I saw for the
      first time
its soft countenance, the raw fleshy jowls
wrinkled and generous, like the faces of the very old
who have grown to empathize with everything.

And I drifted away from them, slow, on the pull of
      the river,
reluctant, looking back at their roost,
calling them what I'd never called them, what
      they are,
those dwarfed transfiguring angels,

who flock to the side of the poisoned fox, the
    mud turtle
crushed on the shoulder of the road,
who pray over the leaf-graves of the anonymous lost,
with mercy enough to consume us all and give
    us wings.

MY FIRST MERMAID

I

In Florida, where these things can happen,
we stopped at the last roadside attraction.

In a small theater decorated with mold,
behind a curtain sagging like seaweed,

a wall of glass held back a wall of water.
And there, in the springs, a woman in a bikini top

and Lycra fish tail held an air hose to her lips
like a microphone. What was she waiting for?

Into the great open bowl of the springs
a few fish drifted. They looked at the two of us.

They shook their heads and their bodies rippled.
Air bubbles shimmered in the filtered sun,

each a silver *O* racing to the surface to break.
We'd missed the day an unscripted underwater blimp

of a manatee wobbled into view. The gray, whiskered lard
of a sea cow or the young woman who sang –

lip-synched, rather – some forgettable song,
her lipstick waterproof: which was the real mermaid?

II

Given the weight of water, nothing happens fast
to a mermaid, whether it's love or loss.

Not like the landlocked life, I wanted to warn her.
But here came a prince in street clothes,

trying to think thoughts that were heavy enough
to make himself sink to her level. His shirt ballooned,

a man turned not to a merman but a manatee.
Yet, in the small eternity it took for him

to grasp her greasy flipper, for her to find
his more awkward human ankle, and then

for them to turn, head over each other's heels –
a ring rolling away, too beautiful to catch –

they lived happily ever after.
Until one of them had to stop for breath.

DEBORA GREGER (1949–)   221

SHOPPING FOR POMEGRANATES AT
WAL-MART ON NEW YEAR'S DAY

Beneath a ten-foot-tall apparition of Frosty the
    Snowman
with his corncob pipe and jovial, over-eager,
    button-black eyes,
holding, in my palm, the leathery, wine-colored purse
of a pomegranate, I realize, yet again, that America is
    a country
about which I understand everything and nothing at all,
that this is life, this ungovernable air
in which the trees rearrange their branches, season
    after season,
never certain which configuration will bear the optimal
    yield
of sunlight and water, the enabling balm of nutrients,
that so, too, do Wal-Mart's ferocious sales managers
relentlessly analyze their end-cap placement, product
    mix,
and shopper demographics, that this is the culture
in all its earnestness and absurdity, that it never rests,
that each day is an eternity and every night is New
    Year's Eve,
a cavalcade of B-list has-beens entirely unknown to me,
needy comedians and country singers in handsome
    Stetsons,

sitcom stars of every social trope and ethnic
    denomination,
pugilists and oligarchs, femmes fatales and anointed
    virgins
throat-slit in offering to the cannibal throng of Times
    Square.
Who are these people? I grow old. I lie unsleeping
as confetti falls, ash-girdled, robed in sweat and
    melancholy,
click-shifting from QVC to reality TV, strings of
    commercials
for breath freshener, debt reconsolidation, a new car
lacking any whisper of style or grace, like a final
    fetid gasp
from the lips of a dying Henry Ford, potato-faced
    actors
impersonating real people with real opinions
offered forth with idiot grins in the yellow, herniated
    studio light,
actual human beings, actual souls bought too cheaply.
That it never ends, O Lord, that it never ends!
That it is relentless, remorseless, and it is on right now.
That one sees it and sees it but sometimes it sees
    you, too,

cowering in a corner, transfixed by the crawler for the
    storm alert,
home videos of faces left dazed by the twister, the
    car bomb,
the war always beginning or already begun, always
the special report, the inside scoop, the hidden camera
revealing the mechanical lives of the sad, inarticulate
    people
we have come to know as "celebrities."
Who assigns such value, who chose these craven
    avatars
if not the miraculous hand of the marketplace,
whose torn cuticles and gaudily painted fingernails
    resemble nothing
so much as our own? Where does the oracle reveal our
    truths
more vividly than upon that pixillated spirit glass
unless it is here, in this tabernacle of homely
    merchandise,
a Copernican model of a money-driven universe
revolving around its golden omphalos, each of us
    summed
and subtotalled, integers in an equation of need and
    consumption,
desire and consummation, because Hollywood had it
    right all along,

the years are a montage of calendar pages and autumn
    leaves,
sheet music for a nostalgic symphony of which our
    lives comprise
but single trumpet blasts, single notes in the hullabaloo,
or even less – we are but motes of dust in that
    atmosphere
shaken by the vibrations of time's imperious crescendo.
That it never ends, O Lord. That it goes on,
without pause or cessation, without pity or remorse.
That we have willed it into existence, dreamed it
    into being.
That it is our divine monster, our factotum, our scourge.
That I can imagine nothing more beautiful
than to propitiate such a god upon the seeds of my
    own heart.

CAMPBELL McGRATH (1962–)   225

TROPICAL COURTYARD

It is a rage against geometry:
The spiked fans of the palmetto arcing
Like improvised brushstrokes in the light breeze;
Like shadowplay, somewhere a dog barking.

Against the height of new and old brick walls,
Confounding stone, transplanted pine and palm
Lift in imperfection, as heavy bells
That would force order fade into the calm

Of azure and a faint scent of musk.
(Is it eucalyptus or just the past?)
There's nothing in this warm, vegetal dusk
That is not beautiful or that will last.

DESTINATIONS AND TENDER MERCIES

Always I am history I must wake to.
— TINO VILLANUEVA

I heard the singing of the Mississippi when Abe Lincoln went down to New Orleans, and I've seen its muddy bosom turn all golden in the sunset.

— LANGSTON HUGHES

THE MAGNOLIA

O flowers of the garden, of skilled and human care,
Sweet heliotrope, and violet, and orchid frail and fair,
Pour out your love to happier hearts; the woodland
    flowers for me,
The pallid, creamy blossoms of the dark magnolia tree!

I close my eyes; my soul lifts up to float with their
    perfume,
And dull the body lying in this narrow city room.
Again I am a happy child. I leap and joy to see
The great curved petals wavering slip from out the
    gleaming tree.

As holy grail, or pearl inwrought, or carven ivory cup,
They stand on bronze and emerald bough, and brim
    their sweetness up;
And underneath a happy child! – O days that used to be!
In distant land, the flowers still stand upon the dark
    green tree.

MARY McNEIL FENOLLOSA (1865–1954)

THE NEGRO SPEAKS OF RIVERS

I've known rivers:
I've known rivers ancient as the world and older than
the flow of human blood in human veins.

My soul has grown deep like the rivers.

I bathed in the Euphrates when dawns were young.
I built my hut near the Congo and it lulled me to sleep.
I looked upon the Nile and raised the pyramids above it.
I heard the singing of the Mississippi when Abe Lincoln
went down to New Orleans, and I've seen its muddy
bosom turn all golden in the sunset.

I've known rivers:
Ancient, dusky rivers.

My soul has grown deep like the rivers.

THE SMALL WHITE CHURCHES OF
THE SMALL WHITE TOWNS

The twangy, off-key hymn songs of the poor,
Not musical, but somehow beautiful.
And the paper fans in motion, like little wings.

HACIENDO APENAS LA RECOLECCIÓN

For weeks now
I have not been able
to liberate me from my name.
Always I am history I must wake to.
In idiot defeat I trace my routes
across a half-forgotten map of Texas.
I smooth out the folds stubborn
as the memory.

Let me see: I would start from San Marcos,
moving northward,
bored beyond recognition
in the stale air of a '52 Chevy:
to my left, the youngest of uncles
steadies the car;
to my right, Grandfather finds humor
in the same joke.
I am hauled among family
extended across the back seat,
as the towns bury themselves forever
in my eyes: Austin, Lampasas, Brownwood,
past Abilene, Sweetwater,
along
the Panhandle's alien tallness.
There it is: Lubbock, sounding harsh as ever.
I press its dark letters,

and dust on my fingertips is so alive
it startles them
as once did sand.
Then west, 10,000 acres and a finger's breadth,
is Levelland
where a thin house once stood,
keeping watch over me and my baseball glove
when the wrath of winds cleared the earth
of stooping folk.
There's Ropesville, where in fifth grade
I didn't make a friend.
My arm is taut by now and terrified.
It slackens,
begins falling back into place,
while the years are gathering slowly
along still roads and hill country,
downward
to where it all began – 500 McKie Street.
I am home, and although the stars
are at rest tonight,
my strength is flowing.

Weep no more, my common hands;
you shall not again
pick cotton.

TINO VILLANUEVA (1941–)   233

ELEGY FOR A MAGNOLIA

Sometimes I dream of her again, in the backyard
Of our brick, stone, and clapboard house in Paterson,
Where the last I heard a black minister was living

With his family. I ring the bell and he or his wife
Answers, but they don't invite me in. Sometimes
I implore them, and even though I am no one

To them they let me in. First I want to see
If they have changed my bedroom wallpaper,
Whose crisscrossing leaves made a net

Keeping me from the kingdom hidden behind
My wall. Is the crystal chandelier still there,
Dangling above the dining room table,

The shadow-caster, the rainbow-maker
My mother and grandmother monthly took apart,
Removing each long, elaborate strand of tears,

Carefully setting the machinery of beauty
Onto a cotton cloth, unhooking each drop
From its delicate wire hook, lining them up

From small to large and wiping them clean,
Then reattaching them before assembling
All the strands on their glass skeleton –

234

Re-hooking the biggest crystal last,
The one that hung alone, in the center,
Like a cold colossal raindrop refusing to fall.

But most of all I want to see the magnolia,
The great old tree standing at the end
Of the yard, its thick lacquer leaves

Obscuring another neighbor's property,
Its huge magenta seedpods frightening me
(As if an unnameable creature were trapped

Inside, ready to hatch at any hour), utterly
Alien-looking, compared to everything else
Surrounding our house. Hydrangeas blue

As dusk, red tulips and apricot roses,
A bed of daffodils, a slender lilac bush
And a row of rhododendrons and azaleas,

Even the subtle well of the purple petunia,
A birch with the legs of a zebra upside-down,
And the sudden buttery-yellow forsythia

Cascading midwinter could not prepare me
For that extravagant surprise, a blossoming
Too quickly turning prodigal and sweet.

Perhaps the only proof that my mother's mother
Loved anything in the world beside her children
And their children (and her husband, Philip Engel,

Who died the year before my parents married,
My mother pinning a tiny black ribbon
To the petticoat of her white wedding gown),

The only living sign my grandmother gave
Of her grief, occurred the day my little brother,
In anger, struck the magnolia, hitting it

With a stick and cutting it so deeply
Its sap ran and glistened in the sun – a wound
She could see from the window overlooking

The yard, where she would sit and watch us
As we played: *The tree is bleeding, the tree
Is bleeding*, she cried. *For shame, for shame,*

It's alive. As she shrieked at him in a voice
I had never heard, something kin to lightning
Ran through me, as if her cry

Were the sap of the stricken tree, its stream
The fine, searing flame of her desire
To seal the memory of what she had lost:

Her mother and her father, her good husband,
Then her brothers and sisters, all of them
Dying of natural causes at home in America.

For though she once referred to postcards
From distant relatives who wrote infrequently,
Then not at all, who were "transported" finally,

No one could tell how much she ever thought
Of those who said they had no reason to go,
Or no way if they had reason, or of the country

A girl of twelve at the turn of the century
Left with her parents for good (*They can keep
Poland*), as she sat in triumph in her chair,

Watching my brother playing on her property,
A plot of land she and my grandfather bought
In 1940 in Paterson, New Jersey, moving

Closer to the river running beside the silk mills,
One owned by her husband, one by her father,
Where she built a proper, unassuming house

Whose border was marked by a tree sacred,
I later learned, to the Polish: the proud
Magnolia Lena Engel loved,

Whose lavish shade we lived in until she heard
Her neighbor of thirty years was moving away,
And the new one would be a different color.

Because of this my grandmother sold her house,
Waiting for a buyer who was white (she'd peek
Between the blinds whenever the bell rang,

Making believe no one was home if she saw
Someone dark through the curtain at the door),
And we moved with her to a flat, rural town,

Returning rarely to visit relatives. Sometimes
We'd pass by in the car, my father pausing
Before driving on (my mother wouldn't look),

Once my brother and I went alone, telling
No one we had gone, walking up the hill
To 19th Avenue, noticing how much smaller

The house was, how immaculate the lawn
And flowers tended by the family living there.
We wondered who they were, I wondered if

They'd let us see the backyard garden again.
Still the wound is burning, for shame.

RHYMES FOR A WATERTOWER

A town so flat a grave's a hill,
    A dusk the color of beer.
A row of schooldesks shadows fill,
    A row of houses near.

A courthouse spreading to its lawn,
    A bank clock's lingering heat.
A gleam of storefronts not quite gone,
    A courthouse in the street.

A different element, almost,
    A dry creek brimming black.
A light to lure the darkness close,
    A light to keep it back.

A time so still a heart's a sound,
    A moon the color of skin.
A pumpjack bowing to the ground,
    Again, again, again.

CHRISTIAN WIMAN (1966–)

DANIELLE

Broadcast all down the Shenandoah Valley
Reverend Billy shouts "surrender
to the love of Jesus Christ will get you there."
His drawl a stream
beneath the words
                    floating the words
his voice goes streaky as the sun
slashing through sumac.

Yammer from Watkins Glen:
"Juan Pablo on the rumble strips
and Allmendinger, wheel on fire."

The signals grow then wane
as exit signs and billboards press
then disappear inside the bright
corn syrup blur
                    where everything
feels dizzied toward some promised future.

Here though (wherever here may be)
only white noise now.
                    And her last night.
Her voice around our clutch
of friends half lacquered on lawn chairs.

240

"From when I was eight I had to suck it up.
When Mom was sick I cooked our meals.
I never questioned this arrangement.
People kept saying pray. Just pray.
And when she died
                    Kathleen and I got tested.
The results were clear:
both of us carry the disease.
I left the seminary.
                    Life was a sinkhole
and I was wild and straggling
and one night
I woke up in a mansion naked.
No one had, you know. I was fine.
Just walking through this mansion naked."

Box stores and crosses on the hills.
An Appaloosa shakes her mane against the purple
mountains tumbling south.
Reverend Billy shouts
"some seeds fall down in thorns and thorns grow
        up and ..."
Shadows of the summits blue
across the stream of cars
still streaked with orange.

It feels so close:
that deepest human space
as she described it.
"From the window I could see
neon I knew was Bourbon Street.
My hands grasped air
then tables and mantles.
At the end of a corridor stood a woman.
And she was beautiful.
Everything glistened: curious and living and
I walked
         by catching myself while falling."

THE BLUE TERRANCE

If you subtract the minor losses,
you can return to your childhood too:
the blackboard chalked with crosses,

the math teacher's toe ring. You
can be the black boy not even the buck-
toothed girls took a liking to:

the match box, these bones in their funk
machine, this thumb worn smooth
as the belly of a shovel. Thump. Thump.

Thump. Everything I hold takes root.
I remember what the world was like before
I heard the tide humping the shore smooth,

and the lyrics asking: *How long has your door
been closed?* I remember a garter belt wrung
like a snake around a thigh in the shadows

of a wedding gown before it was flung
out into the bluest part of the night.
Suppose you were nothing but a song

in a busted speaker? Suppose you had to wipe
sweat from the brow of a righteous woman,
but all you owned was a dirty rag? That's why

the blues will never go out of fashion:
their half rotten aroma, their bloodshot octaves of
consequence; that's why when they call, Boy, you're in

trouble. Especially if you love as I love
falling to the earth. Especially if you're a little bit
high strung and a little bit gutted balloon. I love

watching the sky regret nothing but its
self, though only my lover knows it to be so,
and only after watching me sit

and stare off past Heaven. I love the word *No*
for its prudence, but I love the romantic
who submits finally to sex in a burning row-

house more. That's why nothing's more romantic
than working your teeth through
the muscle. Nothing's more romantic

than the way good love can take leave of you.
That's why I'm so doggone lonesome, Baby,
yes, I'm lonesome and I'm blue.

ACKNOWLEDGMENTS

Thanks are due to the following copyright holders for permission to reprint:

AI: "The Singers." Copyright © 1972 by the Estate of Ai, from *The Collected Poems of Ai*. Used by permission of W. W. Norton & Company, Inc. AMMONS, A. R.: "Easter Morning." Copyright © 1979 by A. R. Ammons, from *The Selected Poems, Expanded Edition* by A. R. Ammons. Used by permission of W. W. Norton & Company, Inc. ANDERSON, MAGGIE: "Sonnet for Her Labor" from *Windfall: New & Selected Poems* by Maggie Anderson, © 2000. Reprinted by permission of the University of Pittsburgh Press. BERRY, WENDELL: "Manifesto: The Mad Farmer Liberation Front." Copyright © 2012 by Wendell Berry from *New Collected Poems*. Reprinted by permission of Counterpoint. BIESPIEL, DAVID: "To Sylvester from Terminal B" from *Charming Gardeners*. Reprinted by permission of the University of Washington Press. BISHOP, ELIZABETH: "Florida" from *The Complete Poems 1927–1979* by Elizabeth Bishop. Copyright © 1979, 1983 by Alice Helen Methfessel. Reprinted by permission of Farrar, Straus and Giroux, LLC. BOLTON, JOE: "Tropical Courtyard" from *The Last Nostalgia: Poems 1982–1990*. Copyright © 1999 by Ed Bolton. Used with the permission of The Permissions Company, Inc.,